DEPRIVED SOLICITATION

(A COLLECTION OF POEMS)

Bengali: BONCHITO UBDAR

Author & Translator:
M. Hasan Imam

Order this book online at www.trafford.com
or email orders@trafford.com

Most Trafford titles are also available at major online book retailers.

Printed in the United States of America.

ISBN: 978-1-4269-6154-0 (sc)
ISBN: 978-1-4269-6155-7 (e)

Trafford rev. 08/08/2011

 www.trafford.com

North America & international
toll-free: 1 888 232 4444 (USA & Canada)
phone: 250 383 6864 ♦ fax: 812 355 4082

A few words:

It is my belief that from the very start of my career as a writer, especially in the rhythm and body of poems, in vocabulary, in expressions, the human life, the daily social life, humanity and human rights issues come straight up over everything and want to stay alert to join in the time stream of eternity, to keep an eye on the life stream of all time, be it the neglected, oppressed, poor human or the cruel power of the oppressors.

Today, I am truly pleased in this thought that the long cherished devotion of mine is finally shaping up in reality through the publication of this selected cluster of poems, the name of which is *Deprived Solicitation* (Bengali: Bonchito Ubdar). While I was living here abroad for many, many years, most of these poems have been written within that time period. With a great hope I have come so far to present my works to you. The works that have found place in this publication cover a period of over thirty years.

At this time junction, I have presented to you a part of my literary works of all those years. To that end, I am conceivably affirmed, delighted, excited and in humble silence, hopeful. I hope through the creations of these time periods, I shall have the opportunity to come close to you for the works that I have endeared for so long. The past ages and the works have spoken and now it is up to you to judge, to slice and to build, if it is to be so. Let the bell ring if it is to save human causes and thereby humanity.

I would also hope that in the tide of this publication, let it tremble, shiver, crumble and finally break down to ruins the workshop of those of the oppressors because of whose terrible thoughts, plans and diplomatic cruel deeds the innocent oppressed, repressed and tortured human of my devotion day by day sink to the bottom of their unblossomed life. Let them, the oppressed, be awakened and rise up with vigor into the tide of life at this moment.

M. Hasan Imam
Author

Contents

"In the little heart, the unending thirst
Not quenched, will not quench, hope will not be fulfilled."

[This was my mom's memory touch
That was framed in glass in village home
Hanged on the beam of sitting room
In my very childhood.]

Recognition

Let me take this opportunity to express my gratitude to Liju, Kaman, Suzanna for their help in typing some of my work and most of all to my son Russell for helping me out in typing many of my works. I am, indeed, thankful to them.

Dedication:

Dedicated to the uplift of humanity
In memory of those-
The human who in country after country
Are oppressed unjustly, are violated
Robbed, deprived, driven from home
And ultimately life destroyed.

In this collection:
The length of time of writing of the poems
Extends from 1971 through the year 2006

Other Published Books of this Author in Bengali

Total of Twenty-Two Publications of which all but Three are Poetry Books

1. *In Search Of Light*
Bengali: Alok Bartikar Shondhaney

2. *In Devotion*
Bengali: Onuragay

3. *In Long Days Path*
Bengali: Onak Diner Pothay

4. *Going Singing*
Bengali: Gaiey Jaie

5. *Different Style*
Bengali: Onno Rokom

6. *Named It A Mixed Taste (Mixed Collections)*
Bengali: Nam Rakhechi Misron Shud

7. *Will Listen One Day*
Bengali: Eik Din Hobay Shona

8. *Just The Other Day*
Bengali: Aieto Shadin

9. *Framed Pain*
Benjali: Badano Jontrona

10. *Flow*
Bengali: Probaho

11. *In The Path Of Poem*
Bengali: Kobitar Pothay

12. *Standing In Front The Dream City,*

New York **(Novel)**
Bengali: Somukhe Dondaoman Shopner Rup Nogori, New York

13. *America After Eleventh September*
(Novel)
Bengali: America Agaru September Por

14. *Suddenly In Different Mind*
Bengali: Hodot Onno Monay

15. *Deprived Solicitation*
Bengali: Bonchito Ubdar

16. *Doesn't Heed Stop Singing*
Bengali: Guaite Manena Baron

17. *Still Continued Asking*
Bengali: Akhono Cholsey Juson

18. *Anchored On The Shoulder of Man*
Bengali: Munober Shioray Nungor

19. *Entrapped Ardent Entreaty*
Bengali: Ubodda Ukoti

20. *Tie Free*
Bengali: Badon Hara

21. *Brightened In Silent*
Bengali: Nirobe Utvasito

22. *Wake Up In Wave After Wave*
Bengali: Torongay Torongay Jagao

A Piece Of Paper

Bengali: Tookrow Kagaj

I am a piece of paper
Lying haphazardly
Upon the chest of the public thoroughfare,
I fly up and down with the slap of the wind
Within a little distance in the air
From the face of the earth.

Again, I wrap-around myself falling on the thoroughfare
My body gets rudely twisted,
The next moment the slap of the running vehicles
Throw me at a distance, sometimes lying on the dusts
And, sometimes again, waving in the air
Like the falling kite with the broken string from its reel
Upon the chest of the thoroughfare with a thud.

Sometimes, under the wheels of the passing vehicles
I am crushed and grinded,
Before I have a chance to breathe
The slap of another speedy vehicle
Lands on me again,
My head goes spinning wild
And revolving and revolving I fall down
Like a sunken drunk man.

Consuming these slaps from every shore all around
Many times
I pass across a little distance
On the thoroughfare.

Once in a while my fate is a little better
After a few strikes and slaps
I fall down and lay aside by the thoroughfare
Where the strikes from the speedy vehicles
Are not unfrustrated,
I keep lying down in a pellucid counting of time
And I see-
The blind speed of civilization in a careless competition
Leave me behind
In the soiled dust or by the filthy roadside
In an indomitable dire desire of senseless speedy advancement.

In dirty layers, I am a piece of paper
By that thoroughfare,
And the face impression of a human-piece
I behold in this path of the world
In the outskirt of this speedy advancing civilized world
Under its feet.

March 1, 2003
Port Washington, NY

Eyes Stolen While In Motion

Bengali: Gothir Mazee Noyon Horon

I crossed this path many, many times
When this tree was little
A baby plant, I have seen its shape
Standing thin,
Few baby branches
Into which peeping through some
Small soft baby leaves
Fresh green are their color
Thin and slim body structure
The shapes are like those of turmeric leaves
In cluster in each side of the leaves backbone
They are connected in a disciplined order-,

In the swing of whispering wind
Whose soft branches
Used to go dancing raising waves in the air
Like an endless playful joy,
For those travelers
Who while passing by
Has discovered this pleasure-mine-,

Again, the slap of some gusty strong wind
Or, in the thrush of some uncontrolled storm
Whose soft body
Have survived the torturous bending

Even after losing some limbs here and there,
I have seen that appearance as well
While passing this thoroughfare
Again and again-,

Because of haphazard striking by some unruly passersby
Whose body was hurt and inflicted
Resulting in loss of some skin and tissues
From some parts of the body and branches,
That little baby plant has grown up
Like a human baby
Witnessing the taste of harsh times-,

I crossed this path many, many times
That little plant now is an established youth
In the swing play of winds it's vibrant growth
Today, has stolen my eyes
Even in this twinkling space of time
Of such a speed of the car.

May 13, 2001
Port Washington
New York

Middle East And
The Drum of Civilized

Bengali: Moddho Praccho o Shower Dumama

Civilized society-
Afflicting its own pride who
Arouse shiver around
In self satisfaction through files of techniques
The stepped over humanity of the world-locality
In the twister of injustices
Are whirling, oppressed
Like snatching away the hearts of human,
They all-
The captain of the ship that imposed deranged humanity
Absorbed in giving directions in delirium wish,
Embracing the injustices
They bid goodbye to human affection
Through the back door,

The shade of world war
Like the shade of clouds
Come afloat floating,
In the Middle-East game, keeping alive
The eagerly destructive human conscience
Encircling the places and nations
Stay in stake of problems,

The belly dance of fun taunting
Roam around
In the village and locality
The claimer of proud civilized world stay wished
The innocent human in this shore, in that shore
In the swirling smoke of international political marijuana
Are losing lives home, family, and close ones
Bidding goodbye to the world
In silent signal in half-closed eyes,

Where is the so-called greatness claim of human?
Like the hated sly cat
Keep quite somber at a distance
Throwing the human
To strike and kill each other
Decorating thy self the king of kings of the world
Their blind selfishness is stealing
Thousands of innocent lives in the Middle-East
They are the Palestinians under suppression of injustices,

Swallowing oppressions year after years
They are common Palestinian populace, innocent Jews
Fall prey in the swing of justices and injustices-,
They are the Muslims of India
Objects of shameless slaughters in hatred religious communal riots
They are in shore to shores of Africa
Human clusters under oppression of injustices,

You are the owner of beginning and end of this world
The civilized society -
Spreading this unwritten propaganda around
You are amusingly watching the fun
Tactfully spreading the diplomatic paw
To see how to keep playing around
Leaving wounded, dead, half-dead
Helpless human lives

Like the cat-play of rats
In this unsettled boundaries of Mid-east,
Nevertheless, just look and see
Like a terrible peace-less bad dream
The foggy human hearts are surrounded
Each day every moment embracing the death,

Like in the king's council
In the "Discovery of Shoe" by laureate poet Rabidranath Tagore
You are playing similar play
That's what it seems,
To relieve the human
From oppression, death
Of these and those shores
Only pick what is at the root of problems,
To save these feet
From the dirty touch of dust
A cover-like the shoes is only needed,
Then and only then, it will certainly fix
The solution of unjustifiable deaths of the Middle-East

April 5, 2002
Port Washington
New York

Chess of Middle East

Bengali: Modho Prucher Daba

Now, the life of human
Impossibly-
The basket of politics,
The favor for humanity, in the face of tremendous oppositions
In severe complexity-
Is looted, booted, wounded, and massacred
Finally chained in the mud of rejection
The sign of humanity is inflicted, bloodied in wounds-,

The democracy of humanity in world politics
Is locked in the knot of getting or not getting votes
Is often, in civilized ruler's power,
The breathing is like going to expire
Upon pressure on the humanity throat,
Maybe in fashion of neglect the world war
Is coming, and coming closer to door-,

That's right, the powerful country like America
Sitting on the back of civilization
Having power of giving gift of life
Among the Arab world
Keeps its friendly country out of debate
In high altitude,
Quietly watching the humanity slips off-,

It doesn't take any firm justice step
Holding the truth tightly closed in clasps
Maybe in sheer thirsty hope
To get the votes-
Leaning head against the throne
In the lap of forthcoming election,
Not yielding in favor of children and all other humanity-,

Throughout this shore and that shore alike
Innocence, they, are giving lives, stream of blood
Because of whimsical games of developed and civilized nations.
In the middle, human discovers itself
As prey of this unjust politics
In the tongue of its glowing blaze-,

Now, the life of human
Is the bait of heartless unjust politics
Cannot find the known path of solution
Keeping the eyes blinded in "touch me" game
Under the fleet layers of black clothes,
The lives of the Middle East swings
In the shedding of blood drops
Keeping the civilized responsible
In the play of focal point of chess.

May 31, 2002
Port Washington
NY

Image Of Reception

Bengali: Shomboddonar Shoroop

All of you give reception
To this head of state
Pour out your heart
Kneeling down in his/her path
And think, your unsatisfied thirsty mind
Is gratified now that you have seen him/her,

You've seen but he/she may or may not have seen
In unmindful blank mind casting floating eyes
He/she has given political timid smile,
You've understood you're gratified
Because he/she has seen you-
His eyes in essence, moves in different directions,

If your love to the
State and all people of the state
Their lives and the security of their properties
Have shown importance and preferences
Then, this reception
Needs to be analyzed and justified,

All the institutions of the state, social nerves
The daily life of human, devotion of social discipline
If gets broken down and destroyed,
Covering the life of majority civilians

If, it becomes the ruined ground of destruction
In every nerve throughout the country
Because of this administrator, the government, and political group
Then, justification needs to be analyzed
The worth of this reception
Is how much meaningful
For all the people of the state,

In leading everyday life
Your country people, when
Locked up in drunk-chain of bad administration
In the process of running their political activities
The general human, when
Get deprived of the value of life and unprotected
And thrown at the bottom-
Somehow staying alive in a valueless, worthless life-,

The worth of this aimless philosophy-less and justification-less
reception
Needs to be analyzed and investigated,
How meaningful it becomes-!
Instead, does it prove a total negligence
Of the conditions of your country people
Upon the shoulders of these organizers-,

Reception needs to be conquered and earned
Under the shelter of administration and political party
Under the wheel of calumny
Not caring of the conditions of human life
Wearing the garland of administration
There, who comes stepping on the
Hippocratic red carpet-!

The stars of the sky, you are the witness
Of these life conditions of this human,
Engaged in the melee of receptions upon the face of earth

These hesitating longing minds,- rise up
With the directives of the stars
Look around-
The picture of innumerable killed and dead
Come afloat in the canvas of politicians
Shining brighter and brighter
Like the impressions of lightnings

June 16, 2002
Brooklyn
NY

Connections Imbedded

Bengali: Deachi Gethe

The blazing tongue of your aspirations
Lasting,- to remove this body and mind
As if to break down and destroy
In eternal darkness
Little by little
The dream castles that I've built.
Sitting in the back of ages, whom
I lifted up
Here and there
Burdened and tired in sorrows, this human villa-,

In the soft red glow-body of the setting sun
I've attached that human's
Picture of deeply oppressed scaling heart-,

The impression of darkness of the night
Passing from layer to layer-
Like all the impure chemicals
Get purified and transferred through modern filters
And get freed to arrive
With the glow of the morning sun
In this deep meditating hope
I placed my step-,

In my body-
The cells get pain attacked
In soundless scream from all directions,

M. Hasan Imam

I know where is the origin of those roots
They want to subjugate me
Bringing crooked strike upon me,
And yet, I am settled in mind
Kept determined this promise
Keeping a firm soft touch of feeling
In the depth of my mind-,

This decaying of human
I long to see being curbed and eradicated
Keeping the speedy time in ratio order

July 7, 2002
Long Island, New York

Term

Bengali: Tarm

I've come to a term with myself
In demand to go ahead,
Not willing to allow the opportunity
To be slipped away
Have to go far-

Life is like a ransacked fountain
Wants to get little rest with peace
Little touch of happiness-,

Sprinkles of happiness come by
The air sweep it away quickly
Before even touching it
The rain of happiness doesn't come down
Only sprinkles drops around
In the flow of life river-

In my mind, I've come to a term
With myself
In the banks of millions of rivers
Those, the hundreds of millions of inhabitants, huts and villages
They all, in the ruined fountain of humanity of the civilized
Sell themselves-
With a hope to catch a little cool touch
In their body and mind

Of the real peace fountain that
Goes floating in the waves of air,
A definitive dream of happy slumber
Didn't anchor
For a lengthy attachment of time
In this spring's deprived villa-

The floating picture of happiness in distant stars only
I've seen have returned again and again,
This time is not a wrong time
Still, why then, mind comes back again and again
Under the umbrella of the civilized
Where choirs of human
In the tune of my song
Have joined in chorus tune
Like the way my own-

Today, it is not the sky with full of stars
Tomorrow we shall meet
With you all again
We'll talk, speak out nonstop
The thoughts of my mind
Whose language is very clear
Not hard to understand,
My relentless talk of peace
Whose strings have merged
In the tune of your life song.

July 27, 2002
Port Washington
New York

Unfolding

Bengali: Ommochon

Between the feeling of each shivering of every moment
The rows of hung balloons
The let free pigeons from the cage
And the dancing waves of their wings in the air
How could this wipeout
The hooli-dance of oppression upon this heart
Deported, the knitted blackness disrepute like a Nokshi-Katha
design
That which in harsh times pulled over
The unmistakable knots of needle or thread,

In the lines of fingers
The way the days and months have filled the years
Picking a day out of those, and
Suddenly observing spreading pleasures
How could it in the roots of sorrows and pains
Raise merry making happiness and pleasure
To distribute pieces of cake
Wiping out the accumulated memories of all the guilt and crime,
The rows of parades and its beauty
Keenly put together flowers and garlands
Coming forward embracing on birthday path
It's the celebration of that so-called moment of birth
Man has given the point of that birth
Filling the tune with attraction,

Where would you hide all the unthinkable wounds to human
In their face, body, and in their hearts
This march of yours, this sound of joy
Is the mountain shape of deception of the moment
In the form of a one day birthday celebration
How much path you think will cross over
In the body full of slashes,
This me, mother, the motherland
In the millions of pages of diary of my mind
In the hearts of multi-chorus

The similar unavoidable impressions of slashes
Stay lay accumulated day after day,
Throughout the day this celebration of one day in colors
Have opened up and shaken the wounds suffered days,

Birthday! They, as administers and powerful
Want to see melt away in the drunken feeling of birthday
celebration
All the built-ups upon chorus of hearts
The humiliation mounting of deprivation and oppressions
Without any kind of accountability and solutions
The silent murmur and noise of sufferings.

(Bengali Independence Day envision)
September 16, 2002
Port Washington, New York

Mischievous

Bengali: Duronto

The heart that lies in the depth of heart
In that pearl-center point
My feelings slowly get shiver and shiver,
An uncontrollable strength, a force
Like the aggression by a dangerous demon
In the lurking darkness of moonless light
Wants to remove me
From the center point of my dearest
Simple mind-
Wants to arouse fungus in my self confidence,

Wordless, unannounced and soundless
A terrible conspirator-
Comes and goes setting sail in front of my eyes
Yet, like a deep magic power
Stay anchored in ever present unseen deception,

In the horizon, in the flying wings of birds
Touch of earthquake wakes up,
The soundless depressed mind
In anger, wants to bring out sparkles of revolt
In the clear courtyard of realities,
The next moment, in the algebra of conscience
Texas scientific calculator wants to arouse
Smallest results, tough complex analysis,

Gradually, a foggy cloud of consolation
Like the sucking of ink from a fountain pen
Lays soothingly in the inspirational center of my feelings,

The conspirator still keeps on
House, home, society, country are under seize
The way arsenic stay sunk in the deep underground
Why the public sound wave doesn't come rising
In the true spirit of Bedouin horse
Whose speed is turbulent throughout the horizon.

September 28, 2002
Port Washington, New York

Deprived Solicitation

Begali: Bonchito Ubdar

It's not that hard to please me
It doesn't need a gift of huge pile of wealth
To pour over in this hand,
I'm, day and night, unmindfully
Continue writing myself in the page of mind
In inkless utterance, light touch of
Finger on lips records-
To please me
Is not that something hard-,

In the life's poetry and novel
Human walks, come and goes in each set
Their image is wonderful throughout the horizon
Some are sunk in luxury
In the overflow of wealth and resources,
In their very door front, some lay down on ground
Extending their hands in pain-,
Some get stuck in the murmuring wind of hunger
And spattered around like the broken straw in the twister,
I'm in a sorrowful mind
Devoted in trying to snatch them
Away from the current of storm,
Only this, that I wanted,
A little sprinkle of consolation
For them, only a little

Sprinkle of rose water
That's what we'll give them a just little cool touch
In that very pronounced moment,
Nothing excess than this
To meet their needs
Nothing to get drowned in the abundance of wealth-,

To read me
Is not something that hard,
Whatever is the rightful due-
Similar to it, just easy going
Things to get by living
Nothing in excess than that
Only sprinkle of peace let go touching
This heart,

Sheltering their realizations
Let this sound and echoes be ringing
Striking against the body of unseen mountain,
All kinds of heart-touchables of mine,
The robbers robbed it all
Striking on my dear fatherland
The extortion and maladministration of yours grew rowdy
In the stick of your ruler hand
You've taken all-
All the ingredients
To survive, holding the label of peace!

A cottage and some food
Equivalent to cover the daily poverty
In the mind and body to cover the shame
And nothing else-,

Valuable gifts, promise of overwhelming wealth
I don't need
You have taken all under your open conscience

In the dumb hooligans of senselessness-
Yet, you know
To please me
Is not something hard
An easy going sprinkle of common humble life
To let touch only.

October 6, 2002
Port Washington, New York

War-Heat

Bengali: Juddo Tup

Hi, Nice day!
Unfolding of feelings take place
With smile in sudden meeting in motion,
Now at the appearance of scorching sun
Don't need to run in search of shade
Now time has come that he's welcomed
Bound in embrace-Not only the arms-
The warmth comfort feelings through the whole body
Could be wrapped around
That's what is felt in every cell
Seething the feeling of satisfaction,

Like the memory of a small piece village
That was left behind
The mind stirs up
At this emotional embracing of the present sunshine

The surroundings smiles up
In the heat of welcome sunshine
Whispers the time of the day, human with
Unbearable feeling does not flee now,

So what, on the other side
Upon many other human
The subjugation and torture of modern armaments stays,

Deprived Solicitation

In this welcomed time of genuinely complying day
There are roarings of injustices-,
Even though, there is no need for shade now
In the bestowing of this sun heat
The heat and thunder from the modern arms
Human need shelter and shade, but
Where will this human hide!

The general human, they're the one
Who become the ultimate sacrifice, the sufferer
Because of pleasure order of the big fellows
The might of arms rose in thrills
The thirst of addiction for blood lost it's
Justice, the eye view mind analysis,
In mad aspirations, the blind he, thinks
He will conquer the human soul
Driving fear sheltering fear in harbor,

The invited day of the forthcoming comfort feeling
Hesitates and pause-
The blinded entangled nation in blind justices
Hope, does not do sudden wrong
Does not bring down the third world war conflict,
The sailboats on the neighboring Mill Pond
Busy competing each other in remote controlled race
Hope, do not scatter on this clear water
The compelling repentance of mystic foreign spell.

October 8, 202
Port Washington
New York

Notes He = He/She
Mill Pond = Name of a neighboring pond

Play

Bengali: Khelo

You, in any way you wish
Can play-
That having no end
Is your play,
In broad daylight, in depth of shadowy darkness
The lives that were caught in
You can crack holes through them
In front of ten other people
Within the knowledge of known people-,

Indistinct covering of behind the scene
You don't need,
Who will touch you!
You're known to all
Like within the reach of hands,
Whereas, you're protected in the fortress that far
This doubt would light up one's mind-,
You may play as you wish
Those who have triggered up
Your addiction to play
They themselves are your play-dolls
There is no worry, no hesitation-,

Without fear, you keep playing
With normal helpless lives

Deprived Solicitation

Ruined locality is the depot of your inspiration
Tormented, wounded human, society, family
Are the mists of your wild laughter,
You can play as you wish
As long as in this play field
It is your absolute control-,

Those who with, you're playing in absolute satisfaction
Melting the copper of injustices
Putting the seal by force upon them
Upon their difficult breath
Dam-caring the time
One day their strength
To take this play of yours
When, will end forever
Your addiction to this play-, then
Will not find a way to run and flee
Million times of asking forgiveness that day Will not save you then.

October 9, 2002
Port Washington, New York

Fall

Bengali: Poton

At such difficult horizon humanity is cursed and befallen
In crying pretension, in soundless shout
Heading to the bottom-
That's what mind thinks
The king of king's eyebrow is in severe turmoil-,

Not valuing the roses as roses
Keeping it's long ruler stick in death throat
He is oppressive, strike easily
Whipping and leaving marks in the back of human-,

In the lurking greed for wealth, he conspires in longest roundup
Arresting the judgment of the sound mind
The blind human loses himself
In the clear wings of the rising evening flies-,
The king of kings in the consumed mist of sweet aromatic
intoxication

Settle in pride
In the crown beauty of the throne,
Welcoming the cloud of satisfaction
Covers the laughing counselors of the court
In the wavy shade of the wind spread sheet-,

In the drunken hallucination, he does not realize
His heartache shall arrive
In the stream of human sorrows
In the seize of laughing oppression, his very doom
In the pleasure fountain-,

Note: He= he/she

January 4, 2003
New Hyde Park, Long Island

Crooked

Bengali: Kutil

What a misfortune upon this human,
Like the so-called heresy
Wrapping the trust in a clown's paper cornet
He is the pilot, in the spoken pronounced words
He seeds the buds of fear
Stealing the hypocrisy by the power of hypocrisy-,

Soothing words are they, of deception
Lightened, aroused thrill, excitement of conquering
Putting fear in his breath that enemy monster
Fingering directives throws the slogan of power,
But where is the enemy, upon what proof
He's enemy!- How, what armaments he projected raising strikes
terrible!

Questions pops up in minds of countless human
Words could be said in the form of statements
That's but a statement, the art of pronouncing words
Can be planted whenever and however wanted
In propagating compelling emotions of sentences
That's not proof but over again analysis of statement-,

Or, in the speechless speech storm
Taking shelter in crooked magic game
In awkward posture pulling the creator
In clothe-less indifference wants to tear off
In the forefront of judgment less statements

In the unseen ledger of proofs-,

What a misfortune upon this human
In the path of oppressive adamant blind power
Humanity detaches in the field, in the horizon,
They've no power, knee shivering makes the backbone
Bend and bend soundless, they within the grasp of power
Stealing the deception by the power of deception.

Note: He= he/she

February 26, 2003
Port Washington, New York

Finger Impression Of Administration

Bengali: Shushonar Tipshoi

In my land, my homeland, the long waited landing
Finally, touched my heart and tears,
The eleven O'clock sunshine of the early morning
Filled my body and mind in embracing
From the very first moment of meeting at landing site-,

At the brightness of pure natural smile of my kith and kin
My overwhelmed mind shivered in pleasure,
Outside the terminal
The appearance of the sights of Bangla
Came rushing-,

After a very long absence
The first meeting of the thoroughfare
Has given the sensation of feelings
In only pleasure and surprise,

Within the old knowledge and acquaintances
Almost everything, with a new identity
Came rushing towards me,
The first meeting of the first landing
From the airport until we reached the house
Has brought the repeated peeping of these feelings-,

After landing and some rest thereafter
In the fallen afternoon of the first day
This thirsty heart of eighteen years
Boarded in that very old well-known seat of Rickshaw
And started towards Bangla Academy
The core of the risen tide inspiration of the then liberation,
And there, at the site of respected and accepted 21st February
National book fare-,

From the moment of stepping into the thoroughfare
It came to mind
A definitive feeling of repentance,
That in governing this country
It didn't seem that anybody is in there at all,
That someone is in the responsibility of this country
This thought mind could not accept
In indiscipline surroundings the reckless thoroughfare
The reign of dust and dirtiness all over-,
The long waited moments of absence for so many years
Were having impossible good times
Surrounding the family members
Relatives and friend circles

Quenching the feelings of the heart so that
Not even a moment could get missed
In this accosting gatherings of time memorabilia-,

Only, at the sight of morning news papers
Face to face with the news
This thought comes crowdedly
Zero safety of the citizenry
Depot of massacre, injustices at full brim
This country is drown in killing spree,
The absence in law and order and discipline
Zero implementation

Brings headache in this thought
That anybody is there in administration here in this country
Will never occur in mind
That could be expressed blindly-,

On the thoroughfare, on the street
No, it's not the downfall of discipline
It's the presence of kingship rule of lawlessness
It will not come to mind that anything of discipline
This nation has ever heard of or even know of,
It's the misfortune of this liberation that
The political parties have destroyed
This golden independence in the heart of this land
Under the feet of disorder and lawlessness-,

Anybody would want to cross the road or thoroughfare!?
Oh Yes-!
Bending the body right and left in acrobatic way
Giving some small or big jumps
One has to cross that road, that thoroughfare
To do shopping or else,

Boy, girl, women,
Small, big, elderly, or minor, for all
This dangerous life and death scenarios
Everyday, every moment, if anybody has to go out,
It is as if though, that
In hundreds of miles of natural forests in Africa
In summer, having no other way out
Thousands of buffalos in herds at one shot
Have to cross lakes infested with crocodiles-,
In this path of crossing for migration
The buffalos have to pass, there is no choice
In the process, some of them will go in the stomach of crocodiles,
The human of civilization are locked in the uncivilized circle
With or without knowledge-,

Deprived Solicitation

Thoughts ponder over-
Don't we have to have any value of anything!?
In this poor country!
Wouldn't we have to give value to their lives!

It's heard that there is administration
And it's also heard that there were governments for ages
The overwhelmed signs of fully known maladministration
Fleshes in the full length portrait-canvas,
The name stamp signatures of rules
Goes sinking and sinking
Like the half closed eyes
Foggy shades come floating and floating
The ruling eyes keep announcement
The ruling names only keep leaving impressions of fingertips.

March 2, 2003
New Hyde Park, New York

A Step

Bengali: Akti Podokhep

Come out of the dark into the light
Right here in front of you-
In one step you'll reach
In the courtyard of light throughout the horizon
That light shall
Wrap you around in embrace-
You couldn't even imagine how dearly
You'll be caressed among themselves,

In this congregation of light, all-
Are human in their own value,
You, in a reasonless hesitation are
Throwing away the invitation-,

Come out of the difficult force of darkness
Those lives in there are decaying in the name of human
Sunk in depth from the human level
The blind power in the worship of blindness
Spreading the attraction of ferociousness,

Come forward giving one step
You'll reach in the horizon of light
Where life reverberates with the song of life
Towards each other human-
Excessive wealth is not there but humanity is

Like the horizon conquering morning light
That which, like the songs of birds
Sweet to hear in shivering pleasure
Spreads around and around
In deep murmuring solitude-,

Only one step
That's all you'll need
Difference from darkness to light,
In the dominating dwell-house of darkness
You are balance-less under pressure
Almost drown under the spell of no wisdom,

Just give one step
Trusting in this signal of invitation
You'll see, you've reached the human home
In this courtyard of light.

March 24, 2003
Port Washington, NY.

In Other Words

Bengali: Prokarontore

They walk, go around
The same way
There is slowness in speed
And again, there is speed too
In the city, in local town, in village
Their lifestyle, their spoken words
Resounds in revelation of their existence-,

There are similarities in types of problems as well
The way they grow up
In the discovery of the center point of knowledge
The infants, the children, cry, smile
Mixing the tune in rhythm-
In every locality in reverberation of the same string-,

In the arrangement of situations the modern equipments
In its similarity and perspectives
Spreads over the signs of varieties,
They move around in the similar style
Like in the same street, somewhere in clear pathways
And elsewhere, potholes and broken faces in appearances-,

From locality to the extended locality
The three parts of water and one part of land
Surrounds the affectionate residences

Collaborates into the shades of the horizon
They walk, move around
In different variations of the same hope-,

Remove all the variations of languages from the face
And install the same word ornaments
The utterance of language
You'll see the differences have sublimed off
They're all same
In a more affectionate closeness
They are all human.

April 3,2003
Kings Plaza, Brooklyn
NY

Under The Feet, Clapping

Bengali: Podotole Kortali

Exactly like this, the clappings
Hip hip hoorah, they got it too
In the presence of small gatherings
In the question-answer garden of reporters,
Those people
Who have gathered
In their close proximity attachments
Have given encouragements in words of praises,

They are only head of states
Have fallen in the waste-drain of history
Finally--
When the chair did not guardedly surround them anymore
From the arrow-pinched of hate of the general populace,
Those who have understood this hero's dirty wrong deeds
Towards the innocent human,

Injustices, oppressions, the violent attack of power
Upon the innocent helpless human
Have come open
When the throne has bid them goodbye
From the worry-free protective shield of armaments,
Now, their judgment is in the
People's hands-
Where foundation is
Upon the devotion of true justices,

Deprived Solicitation

The one who got praises and clapping today
Stepping in the carpets of extreme injustices and wrong deeds
By the support of a very minority people
Tomorrow, he will slip and fall in delirium
The institutions of justices and the people
Shall take up in their hands
The gavel of justice-
All those sounds of clapping and praises will run in secret doorways
To nervously flee in a rapid hurry.

April 25, 2003
Massapequa, Long Island
New York

Have To Give

Bengali: Dite Hobe

I couldn't still give up
That long night's
Open solemn of tightly held dying-cry,
In the shadow of promise, the strong desire of preparation
Got to build this shattered social core,
In the keen guise of terrible authority
The naked meditation of indiscipline
Whose design of dressing
Have brought about the uprooting of normal living life
Beheading the head of citizens security
And raising himself to hail
Wearing the crown of decorative body of fear,

The locality is looted in naked in coordination
The bloodied body of normal path rolls over dust
The habitats are trembling, lives are clustered for mercy
Still, didn't forget that
Long night's strong desire
Got to release them free
From this chained cage,

The sparkles of that promise in hand
Still holding the dazzling sword
Come, step forward--
Let's see the sharpness of the strength of your play.

May 31, 2003
North Merrick, Long Island, NY

All These Times, Simply

Bengali: 'Atodin Shuddu'

All these days I simply have spoken
With the paper.
The pen has continued in its ink marking
Have sowed the garland of words.
The impatient swan opened its wings
And have spread widely
The sound of emotional recitation
With the quite clattering of words
Have spread artistries Like the design in 'Nokshi Katha',
The glittering hopes have spread wings
Throughout the horizon
Filling page after page,

I am the poet and have spoken words
You are the paper, to you
Day and night along-
The running horse of civilization
Which I have stopped again and again
In this path, in the path of humans filled with tearful eyes,

Paper, I urged you
Don't let it go in utter delirium
Leaving behind the majority humans
Who rolls on the dust, whose
Befallen souls are bent downward,

Paper, all these times 1 have spoken
To you-
You have given me company in silence
Within your pleasure you have held up there
All variety collections of words of this pen,

And, you left me ever indebted
To you-
For a long while in the turmoil of time
In the ups and downs of this mind villa
You have extended your heart
To have my writings engraved
Into your chest-
To carry it to humans over the horizon.

The ever-unsatisfied pen of mine
Climbing the top of the heart, ran
From this sunset to that red glow of surmise
With an expectation to check that
Advancement-deprived human's conditions their lives
Are not being toppled altogether.

Paper, all these times I have spoken words
With you-
Today the opportunity has come, I have achieved the right
In this exalted invitational gathering
1 will bring up
The issue of neglected, tortured and fallen to the ground humans
In this noble gathering of talented people of civilized world.

But suddenly, in the back of my mind, I look
Opening the door of the heart
I search and find nothing new in there
Worth saying-
All the tortures, all the oppressions
The peak of the sufferings

Deprived Solicitation

Of different kinds of different size and type
Upon the souls of the human kind,
All of these 1 have said from time beginning to the end.

But then, I pronounce in this gathering,
The running horse of civilization
Into your ears and eyes alike
The deceiving cover needs to be removed
Otherwise, in a civilization without humans
You will be drowning with a struggle going above and under water
And ah! You will be only one to remain.

May 31, 2003
North Merrick, NY

I Am A Sponge

Bengali: 'Ami Ak Sponge'

I am a sponge
Soaked again and again
Into this body-
In this marked shape and size
From time beyond I have absorbed
Whatever I could
Within the power of this body-,

I've squeezed out in flow
Ah! The vessels of their wrongs
In the form of liquid
To soak in again
More of the capricious insistence and
Unscriptural practices
Of this civilization-,
Upon this meager shape of my body
In which the mind floats and mingles together
Surrounding the shape of this whole self
Lying repressed existence-,

This body of mine is a sponge
Ages passed by
Upon this body
I have digested the depot of oppressions and unjust
And have soaked in into this body-,

With passing time, from my sponge body
The liquid has gotten dried
So to say, to soak in more wrongs
Upon my vigorous shouting objections,
Against heavy protests-,

I'm a sponge
I've also tolerance-limit of absorption
There is an end-line to the power of soaking
This heart of mine
Has reached that time zone
I have arrived
At the end horizon of holding power,

I'm letting you know
Those of you took it guaranteed
That it's my born fate to soak
They are in fool's paradise
Roaming around in luring drunken addiction

This is my warning message-
I'm beyond the capacity to hold further,
With little excess, holdings will be broken
All the liquids will collapse
At bottom depth-
In which it is heart to heart
You are mingled together
You'll drown with this golden civilization
Clasped into your chest in alas murmur!

September 13, 2003
Port Washington, NY

It's Late, Then

Bengali: Bilombo Tokhon

This bloodshed, all over the world
Equals to irrelevant unjust strike,
The helpless humans are encircled in complex nets-
Prey of unhindered terrible diplomacy of world politics,
The human life is valueless in value
They drop dead untimely unnoticed
In thousands and thousands--,

Their lives are not within worth count
That's how the social dictators, the head of states
Pride embodied powerful world-heads
In the sharpness of their play finishes off
These people's life-light-,

The society cries, the mother cries
The world-heads are stand-still, lifeless
Towards these life-full lives-,

This scaling off in determining the value of human life
Slowly and slowly-
Will cover the sky
Enclaving a dark overcast shadow,
Inside that-
This dear adoring playful civilization
Throwing black-ink and limestone's in the face of heads of civilization

Will blow the laughter of ghosts
At the bottom of the last boundary
Of the sunset that just faded down-,

To save the world society
It's too late then-
To understand the value of human life.

November 24, 2003
Port Washington, NY

Disgusting Insult

Bengali: Bitochrodda Opomun

You're overwhelmed with pride to possess modern armaments
Whose reins of tests are applied
Upon those helpless humans
On the other hand, the meaning stands
Discovering of machines to kill human
You're blindly insane to get in competition-,

These lives are created by creator's own hand,
In jubilation of destruction
You are continuing to kill,
If you can, show-
Create, let's see
One life out of these
Starting right from zero,

Not using the creator's any tissue, any cell
Create that human life
Whom, your blind monster power
Is destroying with
Your destructive modern armaments
Create that human
Whose growing life and
Nourishment of the body would be from hundreds and thousands
Nutrients foods combined
Not with one or two
Liquid chemicals-.

Create that fruit, foods
For that human whom
You will create
From your own made cell, tissues
Don't even touch the creator's harvests, foods
For your created human,

Show how much power you hold of your blind pride
To that creator-,

I know you couldn't, the reach of your wisdom
Couldn't even touch the far distant boundary of that example
Whereupon, your power pride killer hands
Is not even little restrained
To cover your sinned face
With a huge paw of repentance,

If, that is so-
Your power pride is not for the welfare of humans
Dividing the clusters of peaceful human habitats and dwellings
You can drown this
Human living villa
Under the depth of ruins, and finally
Because of your senseless seizing stroke of fangs
This human civilization gradually
May get to be drowned
Coming down from the peak
To the deep endless depth
Pulling the creator into disgusting insult-,

From where, to get up and come back
Will not be easy anymore.

February 3, 2004
Port Washington
Long Island, NY

Rwanda! Yah, You're Sorry

Bengali: Rwanda! Dukhitoi Bote

I'm sorry, to speak out this verse
Is so easy,- whose depth of measurement
May not be even within close vicinity
There is no connection in this expression
With the real meaning of the word,

So, saying sorry then
One can get by and pass aside, or
It's possible to put mind-attention
Into unmindful look of another work matters,

Humanity, sympathy and caring question then
Is another day's subject to discuss
Might come up just like this
As a curious chapter of a particular different moments,

Inside the mind, there could surface
A birth of a thought, maybe not
Humanity?! It can take a break now
From the vicinity of this villa
Or, in the hot stream process flow of world politics
In the humanity less stages of ongoing politics
The inhumane cruel hands of power there
Quietly flow in the human less sheltered room of conscience,
Yah, sorry! Actually maybe not even that
There is no care towards the valleys of
Millions of human lives,

Deprived Solicitation

Very busy only in accepting salutes
Towards its own power pride throne,

Mind runs only to those
To those helpless, hopeless human souls
In the general public human who are but prey of
Unbelievable words of speeches,

The senseless blind selfishness of world power
Keep closed it's eyes, ears, and minds
Towards the dying cry of millions of
Helpless slaughtered human in this blood stream in Rwanda,
Because, there is no chance to fulfill
Their selfishness, no scope, no fruits to gain
The human lives there are valueless
It's just like daily matter to be slaughtered
The millions of children, adolescents

Boys, girls, men, women massacred
To the world conscience, it rolls in dust as valueless
The three-four months of spring in nineteen ninety four
At time of buds blossom, came general massacre
The spring got decorated with fresh human bloods,
It's not the waking up of buds but instead
In modern history of humanity, it was a
Rising of heart wrenching pathetic killings,
The wise conscience of the world that day
In it's selfishness of inhumane blind eclipse
Was drunkenly busy in balancing the account of profit and nonprofit,
They didn't come forward to save this humanity cause
Didn't come forward to stop that
Inhuman stream of massacre and slaughter,
Ten long years after that, today they are all
Busy analyzing and evaluating those horror days,
Busy are all the medias in their own dazzling way,

Yah! You're sorry!
Power stick in hands, all powers of the world
The continuous unbeaten tools of the media
Yah! You all are sorry!
When the erosion of humanity were taking place
Right in front of their eyes
Not in droplets of bloods
But in unjust stream of bloods-,

There are more blood shedding, today
In Chad of Africa, in Sudan-

There, as well, the same story of being sorry
The unbelievable quietness of the world conscience
Like catching fish not touching water policy-attitude

Did the world humane those days took leave of absence?
These three months of Rwanda massacre?
How was it possible for all powers
To adapt this role of keeping quiet as if didn't know anything
Is selfishness so blind, so cruel, so insane
How could someone make it understand
This exasperation of pathetic cry
Mind runs to those
Helpless, hopeless human
Just regular common people they are
But pray of unbelievable infallible words and utterances.

April 25, 2004
Port Washington NY

Ah! The Helpless Squirrel

Bengali: 'Bechara Kattbirali'

The torn-apart body of the squirrel is lying
Upon the road-
Death is repeating even after death
Getting run over by cars
That has no stop-,

Life is not there but upon life
There is beat up-
Having been slapped by car speeds
Again and again in this path-,
From the civilized human among human
Upon the repressed and neglected human
This kind of repression didn't keep mannerism,

The life-full squirrel is now
A wretched squirrel-!
Upon the thoroughfare, it has
Painted a design of blood by its own blood
The tormented lumps of fleshes are awkwardly spread around

Upon the canvas of blood as if
A modern art has been created,
Like the uneven brush strokes of a painter
At different places high and low impression put up
What could be a better creation
Than this-!

In blood canvases

Stood up modern art of body tissues and fleshes
This world that murdered this century
In it here and there
The outbursts of these scenarios are constantly visible
Where the life of human
Is the life of this squirrel
The transporting vehicles of politics-,

The body of the squirrel
Upon the blacktop thoroughfare
Is getting thinner with the passing of the day
Nobody with affectionate repentance
Stepped forward to remove it from the speedy path,
From the affect of speedy wheels and sun rays
The body, slowly is getting reduced and vanished

Like the day ending towards the sunset,
Thereafter, when the darkness will come down
Upon the busy world-,
In the sparkling light of the car
It will be seen-
The helpless squirrel by then
Has succumbed to end itself,
From the repression of careless human
It has taken goodbye-,

The same way, so many life-full human
Whose life was full of rhythm
Like this squirrel
Has ended and still ending
Falling under the evil eye of inhumane.

September 28, 2004
Port Washington, NY

The Ferociousness of Power

Bengali: Khomotar Hinghchrota

I didn't want to be your enemy
Neither it's my desire to be stamped as your enemy
Whereupon, the truthful voice and claim for justice for human
Is a must for me-,

Look and see the surrounding horizon of the morning sun
Equally dispersed in every villa of human
The light of the creator
You are insulting,
Injustices, oppressions, tyrannize and inflicted violence
Upon the life of general people
Have rendered citizen's life unbearable-,

Their death is an advancing march
The slaughter of sly-diplomatic deeds of your power
The previously well-to-do financial conditions
Now they're broken down and wretched families
The oppressions of your power
Made them street beggars, a circumference of orphans-,

Known as the symbol of technological and scientific advancement
This century
You've murdered
By running endless steamrollers of oppression and tyranny
Upon this general populace-,

In this and that directions, in nations throughout the world
Your blind power
Have made you the roar thunder of inhuman
Your end
Is the strike of a sure just results of your deeds-,

Instead, if you would've given step towards good deed
The tense wailing of human would've been saved
Evading the oppression you would've gotten
The equal partnership for loving humanity,
Relinquishing the ferocious use of power
Like the day-sun of the creator
You, as well, embracing that reflections
Would've gotten respect, cordial affections
Like the way accepting the light with devotion-,

Power is nobody's enemy
Instead, it could be for good deeds for all
A highly valued tool
The inhuman and unjust use
Of power
Makes people ferocious animals
Power then, turn to become a curse
A pain on the weak on helpless human's life.

September 30, 2004
Port Washington, New York

The Wound of Sudan

Bengali: Sudan ER Jokhom

Sudan, another dark spot in human page
In the present modern world
Is an example and witness of conscious-less humanity
In the high peak of enjoying modern luxury
The conscious of this people, conscious of the developed nations
Stay hung like dead With sense or without sense-,

The Sudan is killing Sudanese
The name given is ethnic cleansing
Arab militia, the name
Come running at the forefront of the list
Oppressor, killer and rape crime doer
That it is lascivious,- this name
Is encouragingly known to him
The government of Sudan-,

What an animalism!
Killing it's own kind, own people
Holding the name of Muslims
Defeating even the animals who are not human
Millions of guiltless, helpless people
Deserted their own homes, property and village
Without the neighbors, now roaming around, foodless, clotheless
Hopelessly living millions of children and dying
Upon the sands in the name of tent torn-shelters,

The wise people's conscious of the world
Who, without words, jump over
Upon another country in the name of savior
Roll down the oppression of military power
Upon the helpless human with or without reasoning
They all, biting the head of their conscious
Sits quiet, throwing some wise verses
Gaze at it as a fun-,

Against slaughter of millions of armless Sudanese citizens
There was no appeal, no urgent eagerness
To aim to stop this massacre
No awakening for humanity call
No tension to rush to prevent this human unjust
They all are watching the game
The call for must do duty did not come in their senses-,

When it will strike the sense of selfishness benefit
Then, it has become too late-,

The graves for disgruntled oppressed humanity are opened up then
The wailing of Rwanda will return in their mind

Riding on the back of Sudan,-and
In this Sudan, an engraved plaque will rise up
Calling for neglected humanity
Has gone empty handed
And has instituted hundreds of thousands of unjust graves
Surrounding the inhuman quietness of
All pandits of the world.

November 13, 2004
Port Washington, New York

Suddenly the Play Within Sight

Bengali: Hotat Khela Dristir Shimanai

Today, while on the road, I see in the swing of the air
The leaves on the ground are exalted in play
Come running and adhere to the body of the car
In excitement jubilance rolls underneath
Again, in touch me game, run
Go hide in distance
Gather in circle and sit in increment-,

Sometime, with guard of honor, they
Lead the car ahead
And at other time, come running after the car
In the difference of distance
Get tired and settle down
Fall scattered in undisciplined play fair-,

From the side of the running speed
Sometime follow in competition
With the passenger seated in the car
Out of merry making and affection, sometimes
Come running and kiss away
Wants to stick to the surface
In the body of the glass next to the face of passenger-,

Adhering to it for some distance
With the slap of the wind unwillingly and helpless

Has to let go
This momentary attachment,
And has to bid goodbye from the body of the glass
The faces of passengers that became affectionate
Gradually fades away at a distance-,

Today, while going on the way, I see
With the swing of the air
The fallen leaves from the trees
Are excitingly overwhelmed in play
Alongside, we the few
In colored exaltation
Have joined in the play fair of the nature.

November 26, 2004
Port Washington, New York

Asking

Bengali: Jiggasha

It's in vain, to hope
Yet-
Hope keeps awake,
Suddenly for no reason, on sheer pressure of luck
Like the instant arrival of a big accident
If it is seen at a surprise
In a serene quiet blueness of a speechless full-moon
Some changes, an unthinkable signal-coming of
Somewhat polite submissiveness
A flying fleet in a surprising snow-white carpet
Slowly landing in the open court,

Nope, is this a dream-!

Raising in heart a vain hope
Have given all that offerings of devotions
Boiling in sounds in resounding notions
In bubbles fashion the reddish glow decay of hope,

Is it really possible-!

In the divine body of imagination
Dozing in the arms of sleep, he keeps awake
Placing the eye-arrow in the eternal depth.

December 6, 2004
Port Washington, NY

Free the Hesitation

Bengali: Mukto Coro Didha

Civilization, you don't think
I hate you
Your magic touch around me, as well
Flows nonstop-
With that thought the exalted mind
Came out running and saw
The behold of your power-,

You're improving the human life, no doubt
Near around your touch
Those who flow over your body
You're their worshipper like an unhindered flow
Whenever it peeps through the mind
Pain wakes up-,

There at a distance on the other side
By the broken bank of the ocean
Those who've got the title of being undeveloped and poor
In the complexity of your tactical deception
Their lives are pinned down,
On the top of it, they've gotten this title praise
Your affectionate title surrounding the neck of the poor
In your name became a lengthy honor praise
You bestowed in hanging your gift to the civilized neck-,

Civilization, I hate you
This unworthy verse is only a delirium talk

Deprived Solicitation

Instead, with firm belief take into account
Just the opposite of this verse,
I need you
There, those who have fallen down
You're also the savior in their imagination
At this aim, surrender your gift please-,

Your developed signs-wisdom, equipments
Let reach out in their house as well, those
Who've fallen behind out of neglect,
Your developmental distribution arrangements surrounding an uneven flow
Has brought dishonor, disrespect
Your one-sighted blind speed
And it's bypassing flow
Has created uneven lands
Age after age-,
You're not only the civilized civilization
Come and prove-
This heart is offered bonded to you
With this hope-

In that curve of the forest, behind that difficult hill
The deprived human from complete touch of developed civilization
Are the ridicule of civilization that got you
Come and prove that in their house as well
You've brought the garland of developed life.

December 13 2004
Port Washington, NY

Broken Hope Rolls On Dust

Bengali: Vogno Asha Dhulai Lutai

Like a broken bridal chamber
The people of Bangladesh have gotten into a devastated sand-
beach
The hard-worked body and mind from abroad
Tired, wants some peace
In the touch of its motherland's soil
With a great hope wants to settle down in a home
Upon the chest of this dear land-soil,

Not only a home, he wishes
To start
Some kind of work, business
Surrounding the dream of deep love,

Because of which something good for the country,
Along with an income source for them too to live happily
It'll grow with good management
If someone in the name of government
Extends its hand of cooperation
Without the trouble of bribes and unjust demands,

Or yet, if that mental upbringing didn't come forth
No need to worry, nor any objection to it
As a citizen if only there is security
To life and property,

Deprived Solicitation

Unjust troubles and impediments don't appear to create
Environment to a point to lose life
To this truth and value of senses, the government department
If, obey the manners of law,

The many meditations and hope of this home-comer from abroad
Got hurt, stumbles and falls to the ground
Physical attack comes like an arrow spear
Stumbles imbalanced, tends to fall down
They want to throw him to the bottom of unbelievable depth
Some uncontrolled lawless ferocious people of Bangladesh
Whose outlook is the envy of other's prosperity and good fortune
The hungry look is, whose frame-structure,

In the lawless shelter of Bangladesh, within sight of government agencies
Whose terror acts take place
The life of every human today in Bangladesh is chained up
In the hands of these ruthless hooligans
Animalism is whose daily greediness,

Going back in my homeland, in my own motherland
Will build a home and live happily
This dream of the foreign-lived home-comer
In the fear of obstacles and in fear of facing real incidences
Get startled and halted, falls upside-down in despair
In a condition of utter disappointment the decision comes
In these social and political lawlessness conditions
In the motherland keeping the children along
Is impossible to live,

Many foreign-lived home-comers after trying for a while
Became unsuccessful facing these lawlessness tortures
Where citizen's security conditions are at zero
And flee to foreign land again taking family along
Facing such a situation
A long cherished hope for a foreign-lived home-comer

To settle
The love for the country turns out to go opposite,
Specifically for a foreign-lived Bangladeshi
The risk on his life and property
Is an everyday, every moment's cruel reality,
This erosion of the social frame of Bangladesh
Exits, perhaps nowhere in the world, it seems, even
In the poorest country of Africa
No comparison will be found like this,

The overwhelming contributions behind the root of all these
Lies with the political parties that came in power,

This is only political- political and political parties
Killing and wounding, killing and wounding
The head-slash of innocent human
This is the news of the rulers of Bangladesh
The value of human life here today
Roles on the dust in a difference of time of space
The lifeless bodies lay on the ground upon
The unthinkable ferocious strike of human-named animals,

This is such death of social orders!
The witnesses and reasons of all these
Attribute to the inhuman feelings and actions of political parties
The results of their bad deeds of endless greed
These human-like killer-animals stay under their shelters
Or, behind the scene of lawless eyes,

Can't believe, can't believe at all
How this society of golden Bangla
The daily life of its general citizenry
Could fall in this terrible bloodied time,

Where are the people of Bangladesh
Can't they understand
The calling of their death while alive
The locked chains in their hands and feet
In every step of this society,
Can't they hear, understand
All these burning signals of *Aiyamay Jaheliate*.

December 19-21, 2004 Port
Washington, NY

Time Memorabilia Tsunami-Seize

Bengali: Shoron Kaler Salochash Oboroed

Why are these high waves, what a heart wrenching tidal waves
In a lamenting burst, the shaking up of sorrows
Boiling up at the sight of these dead humans,

Surrounding the lives of your creations
Encircling them, keeping them
Covered with your kindness shawl
What cruel-struck these unthinkable tidal waves are bringing
Destroying these ongoing normal lives
In a heap of ruins,

What a destructive face of your creations of this Mother Nature
Whom, out of love, it has given shelter at its feet
Alas, don't know, out of what resolution
Like a feelingless cruel life-friend
Out from the blue a catastrophic flawless paw
Has taken them down at the bottom
Hundreds and thousands of full blossomed lives have fallen dead
In an unseeming attack
In a few moments of unheard of grave rows,

Surrounding South East Asia and East Coast of Africa
A terrible lamentation of these tsunami attack is groaning
Human next to Human, innumerable, dead,

Deprived Solicitation

In an inflicted wordless sights
In silence, a sudden stricken grip prevails in extreme solicit
The gleeful lives of moments before lay in lap of eternal sleep
Motionless, soundless, lay in the lifeless bodies-ends
Snatching away the grieving hearts of the alive,

Breaking and falling, my heart keeps lamenting
Swims in deep sorrows, goes along with searching eyes
With the dead lying in rows after rows, haphazard
The greatest creation of God, they are
And I repent for those thousands of lives,

No feelings, no signs of life, nobody nearby
No neighbors among these ruins, only neighbor of dead
Whom I'll tell my inner thoughts
Where I'll find consolation,

I'm dumbstruck and watching, all that proud discovery of human
Some're keenly expert though, to kill other humans
To your might they're but toys of children
With a little simple blow of air from your end
All these settled lives could be blown at an instant,

Yet, the helpless human are your creation
You've given them the wisdom and courage to discover
They stay under your shelter and look upon you
For what fault of them you've taken this vigor
Thunder-waves fall upon these innocent humans
In your play house who've been busy playing in glee
Remembering your blessings all along each moment,

Your this little, "Disastrous -Tsunami"
Has, hence, engraved the face of your ferociousness
In a little short while who can spread around
The rage of winds, the indescribable signs of destruction

Loosing in the death-ruins the other members of the family
The left alone survivor, the infant, the boy, the girl
Father mother brother sister uncle aunt grandma grandpa
The uprooted tormented helpless family in the heap of ruins
Those who have been thrown alone in this ruthless rampage
Loosing all the earthly belongings, self esteem
They are now -
Wordless dumbfounded beggars of pathless path
Tsunami, - all these are collections of your destructive game

You've been upheld in the honored esteem seat, worshipped
Now they're backstopping, deserting, and are afraid of you

The survived crying human who lost everything
In the rows of thousands of fallen dead
They're desperately searching for their close ones
The air is full of smell of dead bodies
But that did not keep them away
Going round and around all day
In tired body, senseless feet and tired mind
Nonstop, searching and searching
Ah! What a heart wrenching site to watch!

Day after day, night after night
They, who, have nothing but a tired body
Driven by the pain and sorrows of loosing
Seek the touch of consolation
In the dead bodies of closed ones

If only, could find even the dead body
Still it is better I've found them
The last touch of this lifetime
I could put on their body and mind in flood of tears

Thousands and thousands of dead bodies in every area
No identification, they lay down

Deprived Solicitation

And will fade away without identity
In a heap of bulk at bottom of mass graves
Here there is pushing and throwing by bulldozers
And here, in this death, there is no honor,

Scene after scenes stay attached
And alive, in these eyesights
What consolation I could offer them
What words of hope I could put into their ears
What kind of verses I could offer them to hear
For whom their sorrows could gradually be lessened

That this helpless and hopeless human, who,
After loosing everything, every bit he she owns, now
Lies above all these words-
There is no language, no language at all
No language to offer consolation
Only, standing by their side
Keeping the touching hand on their mind-body
We can join in the chorus sobbing and crying
And that is the only way, besides that
There is no language, there is no magic now

Leaning on these sorrows-in-shoulders
I want to lessen sorrows, remove sorrows
The more I try-
With these ever unsatisfied ink-scratches
The more sorrows remain beyond description,

In 1970 thirtieth November, Thursday night
Surrounding the South Shore of Bengal
Thirty forty feet high tidal waves power
From the heart of Bay of Bengal
That rushed onto the shore and Islands in deep sleep night
Leaving behind a never seen, never heard of
Catastrophic disaster in the then human history

Half a million lives perished in one night
As water recessed-
The smells of the dead all over lands and sea
Up above thirty forty feet high in tree branches
Lay hanging together dead humans and catties alike
Depicting pictures that melt away hearts of the world
The humanity that day cried incessantly in tears in silence

Covering manifolds areas today, the repetition of the same arrived
Humanity cries in silent heart bound tears
The pride stay dead in silence,

This present time-immemorial affliction by Tsunami over vast areas of
South East Asia and East Coast of Africa on Dec 26, 2004
Along with the then tidal waves afflictions surrounding South Bengal
Predominantly over South East Coast of Bangladesh
Are two speechless events of history
This Tsunamic disaster of modern time
In many ways is a heart wrenching event
And the testimony of power of the roaring waves,

Originated from the sea-
This nuclear like water-atom bomb of rising waves
Has dumbfounded the world-human
And has inscribed the influential force of power
Of these dearly worshipped quiet water
Since the time memory of this civilization,

Thus, today, at these tumultuous moments
In this sudden shadow of day light, in heart wrenching minds
Letting your handful wrong attacks float in flood of tears
By the side of this ferocious face of unbelievable power
Again, we stand still by your side for hope of mercy

Deprived Solicitation

You've taken countless lives in this attack, ransacked
Give strength and hope to those-
This helpless human, to bear this unthinkable torture
Whose lives you have rendered uprooted and lost.

December 30, 2004
New York

Not Encircling, Solution Is The Open Sky

Bengali: Berri Noy Shomadan Khola Akash

Go, keep encircling your surroundings
Like an impossible besiege
Until when this little space is left out
A little space through which
Act of inspiration will flow
To stay alive
Through letting expiration-,

You're the pride of one civilized civilization
Your surrounding is cordoned
Made you imprisoned
Your self-freedom, free-flow
The area of your free movement
Within the enclavement has made you captive in prison
Your freedom of speech trembles in fear, breathing stopping
Chained up in forbidden order
Because you couldn't come up understanding, it seems
The flow of your blind verses
Has made the entrance hole-path of your understanding
Impeded and blocked-,

Avoiding the solutions of created problems
In outside world
You've arrested yourself in your own world

Binding yourself enclosed in a little space
You've blocked, cordoned yourself
In this hope-
To save your life in an unjustifiable method
This is not your self-freedom, only a deception
It's an unacceptable trick to keep in limited life process-,

News dances out in rhythm with waves
That you might get hit, in that fear-
So that you don't get hurt
You've entered into this very little living space
But look and see the vast world
Is laughing to see your enclave method of
Self-shrinking-,

If there has to be something
Why you will be hurt
That reason needs to be identified,
Look at this example-
To step outside home, the chance of dust and mud
To dirty these dear feet is a possibility,
To try to solve this problem, plans come up
The whole outside world be covered with leather!
That even does not need, in the writing of Rabin Dranath-
If the leather alone covers the feet
The problem is solved,
You may go wherever you wish
The game of dust in feet will be closed forever-,

If any people has to strike at you
The reasons for that need to be arrested at hand
Thereafter, a complete map of solutions
Placing upon open-knowledge table
And spread it over
Now hello invite all parties

Throwing out and shaking off mental blindness of hypocrisy and
deception,
In the swindle of political cloud
Not getting captive unnecessarily in debate
In open mind to truthfully find the real reasons
That which does not say no in favor of humanity,-and
Undertaking plans without favoritism and eye-siding
You could win
The trust of human
The open world then, is yours, only yours-,

You yourself no more
Will need to keep you as prisoner
In this very little sphere-,
Who will strike you!
Instead, there
The world will come forward and say politely
Come, come you the true knowledge
In our midst is your place
Like the open sky
You're the friend of heart.

January 31, 2005
Port Washington, NY

Fire Signature

Bengali: Ogni Shakhor

Keeping fire the witness in the expedition of signatures
The arousing of conscious jingles in soundless silence

The spiritless understanding of unfed conscious at rousing noise of
hunger
The unseen sphere of victorious horizon beats head to dying

Witnessing the memorized message of lost paths of complex day
Surrounding the smaller body of the weak expedition of Kumbo
Korno

The one eyed solemn victory-drum of civilized in a foreign land
The flag flies in tremble at the scared face of hesitation

Lest the fire-signature of deep angry conscious get aroused
The justice voice of self realization come out through trembling
opening ground

The humanity then jerkingly shivering the world surrounding the
body of civilization
The shame hides into smaller holes the honor sublimes off thin

The greater portion of human in the planet are the sound of cracked
bamboos of civilization
Where it does not patch up floats the decay of humanity

Seeing that lo lo the manly might of human

Bend down holding the head suddenly to the end.

February 16, 2005
Port Washington, L.I.
New York

Immediate Before Spring

Bengali: Boshonter Purboragey

Today even, just before the time of spring
Wet snow is coming down from the sky
In the trees it is the reign of settled complete whiteness
The two sides of this narrow path out of friendship
Bent down to each other's companionship on the air
The trees talk in whisper in each other's ear
Offering greetings of beauty to the travelers in the passing cars
Through this Plandome Road-,

Coming forward closer from the two sides of the road in the air
The trees give the impression of a divine friendship,
There is no sunshine and yet-
In white brightness the world is awake in its own enchantment
They disperse pleasure in traveler's mind's eyes
Whoever can imagine this flood of beauty Like the way the black
bees collect the honey-,

In the spread dazzling white courtyard of heavenly dome
Wearing the wings of explicit white swans
The beseated princess lies on the back of flying swan
At her exalted moments of flying
Giveth the kind of felt awakenness of overwhelmed feelings
Spreading around a touch of mystic foggy clouds,
In the realization cell of that rightful moment, the heart
With sequested quench of warm decor in vivid color

Go unleashing, painting through the heart in soft touch,
Today, this morning all these heavenly gifted moments
This path has tied me
In a very close embracing attachment with the creator-,

After spending some captive moments in this consuming passion
The scorching reflections of the sun, by now-
Has brought another awakenness,
Branch after branch in the surroundings
The dazzling reflections upon the naked body of whiteness
Like the mind captivating reflections of diamonds
Bring about an emotion filled in pleasure
The celebration of festivity of God's divine grace
In this vast mine of beauty
But only reflections run in jingling and jingling
Eyes get scorched amidst confounded state of mind
In the tree branches, in the body of vacuum
The exalted mind jumping up wants to float
In the naked wings of dazzling sphere-,

Not being gone to some distance yet
The amazed mind sees the heat from sun ray
Has increased the temperature within sight
Because of heavier weight due to melting snow
The held beauty ornaments are falling down slowly
From the tree branches
And lies on the ground upon the chest of the path
Like a broken hope in a scattered surrounding-,

The decorated beauty that were hung on trees, slowly
Fades away in extinct
Suddenly, a thought of separation engulfed the feelings
Putting in the rope of repentance of losing it-,

Deprived Solicitation

Painting in mind an unbelievable picture
The extraordinary scenarios transforms into just ordinary look
Perhaps with this promise,- raising the message of hope
We shall meet again in this villa

And we'll come back in decor in layers of waves of beauty
At the door of human-
Entering slowly in the dwelling vessel of heart's recreation
And placing this signature-
Flying by spreading brightened sphere.

March 12, 2005
Glen Oaks, Queens
NY

In Terrible Vastness
Bloodied Human

Bengali: Rudro Chorachore Roctacto Manov

Life where fading, dry
Language there dumb, sickly
Distribute hunger, famine in lands over
The blind arms of power raised high in bloody eyes,

The repressed helpless human flee
Leaving their own home, into desert
The rushing strike of flying sand
Hurts in eyes and face of sickly human,

There is even no way to escape, helpless life
Strike of armaments and sand devastating everywhere
Life falls down in the dryness of desert
In disease-afflicted eyes and faces, the flies settle down,

Life fled and came here in this villa
That they will be safe from attack
With this hope embraces the hardships
In the shore of body and mind,

Fled from arms attack yet attacked by disease
Dozes in the shelter-tent, life in confusion
Day by day slips away
The fled beautiful life drops dead suffering pain and hunger,

The pride display of power at human bank
Avoid away in shameless role
Under intoxication of political marijuana
Throws cluster of smoke clouds in swirling circles,

The powerless United Nations swims helpless
Keep going counting in thousands and millions
Of dead and hungry human's pathetic conditions
What to do cannot find clue,

The cruel horse of power runs
Aiming pinpoint at the chest of human
The planet inhabitants are busy seeking their own means
In the sickly hurriedness of selfishness,

The oppressed human rolls on the ground
In their own house, in respective villas
Or, in the self-seeking courtyard of foreign doors
Blood in imminence, freedom royal crown on head.

March 27, 2005
Glen Oaks, Queens
NY

In Unsecured Song Become Deprived

Bengali: Behotogane Bonchito Hoi

With how much care and safe-guard, I kept
This petal-
Whose body is covered with fragrance of flowers
Like a keep-sake mind
Devotedly trying so that nothing could hurt
The body of this petal-
Yet, somehow, like a sudden lightning
Overcoming the carefully guarded seventh vertex
Hurt strikes, reaches here-
In the guarded sleepy body of care,

In a moment, the dream-bridle that was
In an intimate embrace in the wings of enthusiasm
Becomes distressed in grip-
Then and there, the unuttered invisible marks of wounds
Like suddenly surrounding the sky
With unannounced shades of clouds
Overcasts, floats around-In the body of strings of clouds
So like so, that it's like Making fun in a vain composition
To the wounded bird of an arduous meditation,

Deprived Solicitation

Not angry but get pained
The built castle of hope,
The mindbird in the quiet snow-white wings of swan
In a promising try to post the flag
In an unsecured song towards the path of North Stars
Attaches it in an embracing prayer.

April 9, 2005
Glen Oaks, Queens
NY

Poster

Bengali: Poster

The path is strongly cemented and built tough
Nobody walks through this path
The vehicles pass by the side
All day long through the night, in abundance-,

Seldom, anybody would be seen here
To walk pass this path
This walk-in path
It would be seen that a certain distant sweet melody, or
A high society's dwelling or estate
Suddenly, as if, has stopped here
The movement of life, that's why, is empty-,

Small pieces of stones and broken concrete debris
Scattered pieces of garbage
Little by little have gathered and accumulated
By the side of this well-built path
And have raised the signs of another dwelling of habitants
Soundless habitants they are all
Like the soundless banner
On the face of modern civilization
What could be all those languages-!
In those pieces of stones, debris and garbage,
In the collectively gathered places,
Different types, size and colored stones,
More and more pieces of garbage get accumulated

This kind of collective gathering
Surpassing the boundary of city, town and even beyond that horizon
Have grown in the same fashion
The same utterance, the same banner
Soundless banner-
Raising their heads leaning against the vacuum of the sky -,

The frowning of civilization in neglect play
Passes this path and leave
Perhaps cannot understand
This will be its disgrace mark
This is its demise.

April 18, 2005
Port Washington, NY

When They Will Know

Bengali: Kokhon Janbe Tara

At the peak of realization, the conviction of distressed human
Certainly engraved, awaken surrounding the lion-seat
They all speak quietly in sphere
Embraces the fire of burn at the rising position
Unseen but yet present in brightness
Like the quiet flow of bloodstream,

In my utterance in my songs, surrounding the body of my words
In the stream of writing in my utter less flow of words
They speak nonstop
Walk ahead covering in keen attachment
Pull and hold me close
As if, in this promise that they will never let go,

Can reverberate with the tune of song
Such is the right has proclaimed everywhere
They give tune in my song
Float around becoming the melody of tune
They bring awakeness in the link-splure of ether
And yet, they don't know, can't hear my utterances,

I'm awakened day and night at their humming sound
They don't know they all keep me awake
Surrounding the bridal-body of my devotion, it's their whisper
That I couldn't make reach to them even today
Their ever present illuminated stories are surrounding my body
In my word-song, their oppressed neglected life,

Keep awake to establish the remedy sought after
They stay completely unaware, unknown in the shade
From corner to corner beyond the horizon of the globe
My heartache is awaken in relentless thought
Where, when and how this could have reached to them
The talk of their presence is in my all day rising to setting,

How could this be reached to their door
The soundless verse-storm stay awake for them
The humming of word-birds of my austere
Many ages have past in vain desire
The mindbird wakes up and says, then anchor this time
The sunmessage of devotion through difficult path to home of
distressed,

Let them wake up like the evening lamp
Light will lighten up in the surrounding darkness
It will be seen, in the remote horizon of the world in designated villa
The brightness of that light has reached
Now, there is no darkness, gradually it seems brightening up
All around, the demand of writing showing up in its own style.

April 24, 2005
Port Washington
NY

Jury Present

Bengali: Jury Upsthit

Room number five
You're seated in the chair of jury
Some other jurors are also around
All are silent-
Many are attentive to the books or newspapers they brought along
Engaged in running eyes over them to search and research-,

Two O'clock hour will ring up
Court officials shall arrive at designated time
You're seated in the duty of a juror,
In that criminal stand wearing good people's dress
Eager to give impression of a descent person
Is the monster of oppression and torture upon human-
Whom, very easily, with finger directive
They can identify-
Those humans who have fallen behind
Today, they are absent in this court
They're not here but you are
A heavy responsibility upon your shoulder -,

You've stood up to show respect
The judge has taken his seat,
The justice balance stands up at the distance between the judge and
the criminal

In the distance between you and the criminal stand,- trembles
The pronouncing of truth of oppressed human and the cruelty of
that monster-,

You're a juror, the judge of judges
How much power-courage you've held in this chest
To speak out the truth-
Upon the finger directive of that power influence and terrible authority
How much clarity of arduous austerity you've held in this firmness
To send the oppressor to exile and to banish
Today, that very test shall take notice in this presence-,

The victory of the oppressor is but the decay of civilization
Your directive signal shall dictate the writing of that verdict
In this court, in the footstool of civilization,
How deep and wide is the love for human
That testimony shall show up today
In this juror chair who're seated on it to act.

May 9, 2005
Supreme Court
Nassau County,
Long Island

Blossomed, In My Garden

In my literary garden
Blossomed are countless flowers, in millions
Every spot of this front yard is full
They have no language-, only
Vastly spread out in colors like meditation,

In my garden, blossomed are they
Like a quite serene attachment
They place their eyes in this elated voice
I speak their unspoken words, that's why
In the quite sunset time-
They call for me-
So I can let reverberate my tune afloat
In blue vastness
Surrounding the flow of waves into the air
So that, in all sea and lands embracing this planet
My tune reaches the eternal sphere,

In my garden, they are all adorned
In this greetings of hilarious colors
I'm but a burned literary soldier
Keep loving them in utter sorrowful pain
Hear their soundless talks which was
Formatted for me in pronunciation,
In shower of languages-,
For these blossomed flowers in millions
In my garden, if anybody

Has still any feelings left in their heart
And that feeling is still alive
Like the look of a flower,
They will understand that language
In silent pronouncement that reads to me
The gist of inner meaning-,

To live their life, the very essential
Minimum requirements needed to support,
That I'll try for these, in that hope
They have blossomed in my garden
They themselves have brought this height of hope
And I, with unrejected emotions have lifted them
In the sorrowful pain of my heart
Decorating, illuminating them in my garden

From that moment on-
They're the decorum of my garden
And has fulfilled the eyesight at heart rending care,

Each and every blossom of this garden, thus
Is the creator's unwritten unwillingness-
The message of inequality-
In my garden, so then, have gathered
The awakeness of those emotions of
Millions and millions-
The loud voices of these pain-filled combined languages,

Starting from my front door, they are
All awake-
Each morning and evening I see them
Think about them, silently sitting in
My chair in the verandah
Bring them up in my thoughts, and
Then, I keep talking about them
In writing through the ejected ink

Of this pen-,

These blossomed ones in my garden-
They are nobody but those
Neglected human, they're tortured throughout the world
Rejected, deprived, illfully suppressed human
They are the loud message of my garden.

June 7, 2005
Manor Sands Pharmacy
Port Washington, NY

In Tide of Questions Bloodied Child

Bengali: Proshnobane Roktucto Shishu

In a rare moments of the history of human civilization
That this dark page has to have been written
Not in colored beauty but in shameless bloodied word,
Tied up in an inhuman blind belief of addiction
That this considered to be even worse than animal's deeds
In a society different type of people like inhuman
Get caught up after their deeds come in public,
Again, in the guise of man many inhuman when
Get entangled in animal-like deeds,
The shame of holding the dark spot, then, turns unbelievable
And hunts the conscience in deep depth,
Man's this civilization then, looks for ways to hide
Tries to avoid the heat of dark spots
Hiding the face in the dark corner-,

In the black society of South Africa
The unbelievable news spread
Life killer AIDS disease
Has brought death countless in millions,
In one corner of the civilization this destructive sign
Threatens the general poor generation after generation
And are in the face of getting extinct
The world is coming forward

To face and prevent that destructive force
Even though the help is coming in too late
The ringing of this coming slowly getting awaken
When this black human society of Africa
Lies in death-lap
An unfortunate pathetic scenario has come to shore-,

In such heart rending moments of realization
This dark chapter in bloodstream came in this land
Those AIDS patients got in a landslide of
Raping small children in a way like defeating animalism,
The cruel hand of unbelievable disrespectful blind belief
Jumped upon these children
At least that's what is heard-
That,- raping children cures the AIDS patients
This untrue blind animal nail's ferocious strike
How that soft child will bear-?!

In such unacceptable oppression entangled moments
Why the creator didn't punish those monster like human
Why the earth didn't open up into two
Upon the unbearable cry of victim children,
In the neck if this civilization
That's what has become a flower garland today.

June 16, 2005
Glen Oaks, Queens
New York

I'm A Bubble

Bengali: 'Ami Aik Bood Bood

I'm but an unyielding bubble of a fountain
Instead of breaking apart in discipline
I advance, - lean forward
And want to see which soul which king
Which rich which powerful
Had thundered their seats in utter pleasure
Out of such enjoyment as
To see me breaking apart,
That's what makes my guilt-
And that's why I'm called unyielding,

Those who want to have piece of mind
In seeing me break apart
Many among them are not in guilt
May be not, -but
That's not the end of the depth of meaning
Why I lean forward and advance,

I want to see those, making sure
Who, indulging in that pleasure
Destroy at ease
The right of general populace, their property
Who, in cunning betrayal, in deceitful complication
Encircle the life of innocent common people,
They're hateful, keeping their face as normal
They tie into them the heart of inhumans
And then, want to flip over in pleasure

At the sight of me, breaking apart-

It feels intolerable to me
Breaking the disciplined line, my mind
Wants to jump up-,
Catching hold on them in a single leap
Identifying and then handing them over
To the oppressed human of the world
Where they will be tried in open court
Thereby, shall survive the innocent general people
The colorful propelling of bright letters of liberty
Like a poisonous arrow
Would pinch in their face and eyes
Who might shelter the same wrong again
Upon these luxury less innocent human.

Face to Face

Bangali: Mukabelai

I am but a very small drop of this vast creation
A general people
Holding tight an ingeneral promise
Walking the path towards the rising sun that brings results
In this path, clusters of garlands of goodwill
Are not waiting in embrace-
The beauty of promise are not spread in affection either,
In this path, the unkindly, unopposed terrible authority of power
Often in shameless nakedaddiction
Go roaming upon the true dues of the weak,
In this path, the civilization named opportunist's abominable practice
Encircle the home of the weak indoor and outdoor
Ransacking and ruining right and left
And then deserting
Pinning into their mind the directive threat of fear-,

In this path, the countless strike of
Nails of ferociousness
In the veins and nerves of helpless human
Shed lots and lots of blood-,
Thereafter, under the mask of hypocrisy and pretension
Marches undue try to pretend to be a good man-,

In this path, under the hidden grievous lurking of imperialism
The general poor people's country in different sphere

Fall prey in unkind hands of raising snake serpent,
In this path, the lava impression of oppression and torture
In country after country upon the skin of the poor
Go cutting deep wounds-,
Whereas in this very path the sights of developments of civilization
Raises surprise startles-,

Originated in golden Bengal, the flow of my bloodstream
Slowly opens up to let know
The deep apprehension of trouble in this path,
The government of own race rulers, the politicians with no hesitation
Shamelessly looting the wealth, stealing but not stopping oppression,
With one difficult determination, I'm walking through this path
To face the great power
Whose systems of oppressions are almost countless
I know I also have power, the power of the people
Like the power of clouds that can put even the sun behind.

July 8, 2005
Port Washington, NY

The Arrow Shooter

Bengali: 'Tirondaj'

The deceitful heart in expertise
I have seen, in decay night
In corner after corner of civilization
Where humanity in silence
Tumbles and drowns
Fall in darkness in utter negligence,
Busy are the intellectuals
At the foot of civilized
The arrow shooter from the shade, aiming at pinpoint
And preying the heads of humanity,

Succumbed to the luxury of the rich and civilized
The intellects are overwhelmed,
Not seeing the arrows passing by all sides
Towards the target
They are under the fog of sneaky deceits
The path speed of arrows
Are not noticed -,

Or, is it that
Just avoiding a little
Eyes, ears and mind are kept away
From the aim path of arrows,

Out of utter wordless pain
In the veins and capillaries of repentance

The biting conscience in these thick skinned bodies
May be, does not work-,
Worldwide that's the outburst of scenarios
Seen everywhere
The arrow shooter still stay in course in aiming.

July 16, 2005
Glen Oaks, NY

The Nation In Decay

Bengali: Obokkhoe Jati

The decay of humanity shades blood here too
In hundreds and thousands
Countless,-daily
In this Bangladesh that very signature
Have gone coerced in the stream of veins
The injustices, unjust oppressions in the society
Its daily wearing-,

Countless human lost their lives
Losing everyday outside the news,
The world does not know, in every nerve of it
Injustices, forceful occupancy, shameless power play
All kinds of security of the citizens are equal to laughingstocks-,

Where everyday life is intolerable shiver
Going to the street with little extra money
Brings fear every moment in body and mind
Body startles at times-,
Coming out of a bank is the same helpless feelings
There is no guarantee that in intact health
One would come back after market shopping,
In the market, in the street, in Rickshaw and in own locality
In any place-
Sudden attack, face-to-face with hijacking
Day to day this unfortunate mind crying

The general public life in this independent country is the jail of sufferings-,

In social life, in offices; in government offices
The shear absence of implementation of law and order from police department,
The downfall of morality where, has anchored in its roots
In every sphere, in every nerve of society
The sign and hope of morality's influence, as if
Has been buried under grave-
The daily threat and hijacking worth society
Has, therefore, taken shape-,

Safeguarding own land property and building house on it
Is equal to extreme suffering in the hands of illegal donation mongers
The zero level of citizen's security,- equally
Letting down decay of the morality to its extreme bottom
With help of all political parties that shared power
The social life of golden Bangladesh has come to bottom of sufferings,
In own country, own roads, own home
It's not an utter scarcity but absence of security
Has given the citizens peaceless indefinite trouble and confusion-,

The rows of buildings are coming up touching the sky day and night
The social life, citizens' life, are going down
Sinking in the deep dark indefinitely,
The first condition of all the citizens are the citizens' right
Where, one's own life, all moments and property security and social life

As well as morality has gone astray-,
The development there would be judged on what basis, on what condition
What else are left for a nation!
All these years after it's liberty and independence
All decays are brought by all power attaining political parties,-

Deprived Solicitation

By treating the life where the value of life is
Only assault, hijacking, killing
General citizens' life and property are without security
Society and the talk of development there
Is meaningless, only insane, unreal and enjoyment less.

July 31,2005
Glen Oaks, Queens, NY

Conspiracy Afflicted

Bengali: Shorrojontro Kator

Today, I'm surrounded from all sides
Prohibition is set on my steps
Beyond my own sphere
The mannerism of civilization in the guise of abominable practice
Surrounded me-
Obstacle has been installed on the flow of my pen
They want to put in cage the expressions of my feelings-,

They want to render me companionless
Throwing me in the quiet villa
So that, those they are unable to know
That I speak their words
So that they cannot hear my clear poster voice
The seizing by a soundless conspiracy
Wants to separate me
From my human connection with them-,

Whereas, is it possible to obstruct
The power of sun and defeat it,
They are the group of shallow wisdoms, party of fools,
Who can raise hindrance against the power of humanity!
That it is the tide made by creators own hand
All wrong deeds and conspiracies shall diminish immoral practices.

August 9, 2005
Greenville, Long Island, NY

What is this Game

Bengali: Ai Ki Khela

Was this the fate of these people!
They are the people of this Bangla
The brave independence loving people of Bangladesh,
Very ordinary people, in lungi clothes
In the beginning of the month-
They are the people who live counting day to day,
Buy one cloth and start wearing-
Not to put it aside for good time
Time to buy another one comes when this one is torn
Children and family are also attached in the same formula
There could be some exceptions here and there
But stay-
In the closest arena of that math outcome
The arrangements for food is, as well, it's repetition only-,

In many other countries, in the same style around the world
This is the life-
This is the world of wealthy civilization-,

Living in this civilization
The life style of the wealthy is unknown to them
The conditions of the dreams of liberty-
Of the life in advanced higher standards
Have only deceived them-,

They've got independence
But didn't get higher standards of life
They've got independence
Didn't ge(: good arrangement of food and clothes
They've got independence
Didn't get uplift of their conditions
They've got independence
But have increased worry for children to walk in the street
They've got independence
Didn't get rightful conditions of a citizen

They've got independence
Didn't get security of life
They've got independence
Didn't get worry free conditions to walk in street
They've got independence
Didn't get the honor of life
They've got independence
Didn't get better arrangements of education
They've snatched away the liberty
Didn't get even the littlest right of a citizen-,

They are the people of very little expectation
Who get satisfied with very little
The political parties of all powers
By misuse of power-
Have drowned the end to all expectations of this people
From the moments of start to gain fruits of independence
Their hopes collapsed
By pulling the end of moral decay of the nation-,

Deprived Solicitation

The people who got entangled in this system
Are passing the time like senseless without reactions
Coming to this end of time there is no sign of change
That could catch the eye-,

Helpless citizen suffers hopelessly without crying
The development of conditions is that of knowing of arrangements
The absence of this idea has brought obstacle
In the advance of the nation
The citizen hesitates, will they see it
Even in this lifetime
The hope of enjoying fruits of the developments after independence.

August 11,2005
Glen Oaks, Queens, NY

Shrinked In Pain

Bengali: Bedonaie Shonkuchito

Upon repeated use I'm now reduced
I don't have the beauty I'd before
The whole body has succumed to degrade untimely --,

Shrinked over pain I'm a reduced sponge
Day after day-
In their hands of repressions and unwanted wishes
I' ve exhausted myself to the extreme
There was no other means for me
And I didn't see any other place
To be sheltered upon-,

All these careless usage of me
Starting from the kitchen
Here and there every where
Throwing me in careless order,
At anytime in the clasps of their hands
Squeezing me in a way
To the point of loosing my breath
Some how I manage to keep myself alive
And I get to survive for this time
From their chained oppression methods -,

Reduced by pain I'm a reduced sponge
The earlier healthy picture of my body
Is almost gone in the present context
My body has wrinkled and

Deprived Solicitation

Has taken a hardened structure
My skin is brittle dry and
Gets broken for no apparent reason
In the discolored shade the natural texture
Of the skin
Is giving the impression of a sickly body -,

Shrinked in pain
I'm a shrinked sponge and
I keep upheld
In the path of this world
The reduced face of shrunken human
Rendered by the weight of pain --,

In oppression, repression and neglegance
In the tide of illfed power of
Political diplomacy of the civilized
Those of them who have taken my resembance
In an unresemblance way
They -
In their upheld expressed face of sorrowful pain,
Are rounding up themselves, pulling the oil mill grinder
Attaching them within the name of civilized
In the planet
In the crowed of named-human

Burned unparalleled in their own self
It is their story
That is engraved into me
In this shrinked sponge

August 25, 2005
Glen Oaks, NY

Brightened in Identity

Bengali: 'Shonacte Odhvashito'

In both sides of the backbone
It's the symbol of struggle that
Surfaces out in lines in fashion
And reveals the announcement,
In the cover of hardness peeps through
Those identifiable decays
In lands after lands
They are the identifier
Of the witness of the ages - ,

The march of struggle of the chest
In their bodies -
Are in resemblance with the struggle of the back
Vividly stay surfaced in parallel design
Like the back of crocodile keeps floating
In lakes, marsh lands, and water - ,

In the dazzling lightning of
Overwhelmed luxury of the civilization
Those floating get shivering startled
Within the site of sightings
Like the sudden blinding click of camera
At dead of night - ,

Awaken, they are -
At different parts of this planet
In hardship, in difficult time and life
They push the civilization forward
Towards the place to engrave the name
Not their own name -
But the shameless wealth exuberated name
Of this civilization
In the arms of which hang
The diplomatic dirt of politics
Of this wealthy world -
And the finely divided repression
By virtue of which
That struggle in both sides of the backbone
Take birth year after year
In country after country
Age after age - .

September 11, 2005
Glen Oaks, NY

Protest

Bengali:Protibad

Today, at this evening sunset hour, I've only one protest
Only one perseverance to overcome, one high criticism
In a foreign land the political parties of Bangladesh
Break them down, crumble them into pieces announcing prohibition
Put to the grave of all quarrels-,

Better than this, tightening up your Lungi
Hei, play Ha-du-du
In a foreign land let the foreign society see
In a disciplined way keeping the breath how
People from Bangladesh come back to its own court
After touching the opponents in their court-,

The politics of Bangla soil
In a foreign land is profanity and needless cliques, factionalism
Which has no value but a prideful capricious claim
Meaningless show up of pretending leaderships
With or without knowledge an unnecessary hue and cry-,

The benefit is reaped by the nasty politics of Bangladesh
Inside the country they are the heroes of mischievous deeds
Coming abroad they turn into country lover leaders
The insignificant party leaders at abroad held on head the reception plate
The flower basket in hand in humble pretension
Like the begger pouch of flattering-,

Better than that,- you throw that
Rotten Katha of inland politics
Hold high in a foreign land your own worthiness
The society shall take shape by the power of character
The name of unity there lights up everywhere-,

Today, in this evening sunset hour, I've only one protest
At the heart of all party fissiparism
Hit, bring a strike-
Bring rain of destruction after dissimilation
The root of all evils is the mask of all political parties.

September 14, 2005
Port Washington, L.I.

Notes:

Ha-Du-Du- A local game played in holding breath
Katha-- A kind of local comforter sewn with fabrics
Lungi- A kind of wearing-cloth

The Moment of Breaking Patience

Bengali: Dhorjo Vongo Logon

I've built a dam of patience
At the brink of patience
In quiet solitude
In this Bangladesh-
The inspiration of many unknown conscious in silence
Fall down lifeless in unknown sphere
Through the advancement of whose influence in this land
Perhaps, would have survived crores of people
In their own life setting villa
Keeping the citizenry's respectable place,
Son, daughter, family and relatives
Would have grown up and embrace the life
In their successful life-sail with smiling face-,

It's their misfortune that the opposite has happened
That's why the low feeling of life
Rendered an unpleasant spending of days
In the circle of unjust and atrocities,
There is no protest in the liongate of voice
The signal of inflictable fear-directive terrible authority
Dances in ferocious laughter
In naked intoxication of all the
Power held political parties-,

The disrupted broken society, human only dozes
At the brink of dizzy feelings of self-consciousness
The intolerance have fled from their human realization
Boundary line-,
I think and think over
I've built a dam of tolerance
At the brink of patience
In quiet pursuit
In this Bangladesh-
To record that very moment
When the rise of their intolerance and the breaking of the dam of patience
Shall have taken place
That's why-!

September 14, 2005
Port Washington,
L.I.

Competition-less

Bengali: Protiddondita Benin

It stay fallen on the floor on my kitchen bed
Snatched away my eyes,
Returning from office, I'm seated on the chair and
About to open my shoes,- right then I see
Healthy as the full grown cells of an orange
Like the very attractive beautiful lips
Shaped in one lap
Raw-fresh green infant leaf
Throwing a surprise look
Who's just dropped from the stem
Of that tall standing plant touching the sky light-,

Didn't have chance to step into full-grown phase
There was a promise to bloom
That only became worthwhile-
To grow and to glorify, that promise-
Didn't get to be written
That's why it has stolen my attention,
That it came,- this announcement
Left known in the air in this solemn quiet courtyard
Kindling a magnetic-attraction-color of delicately soft uncommon nature,
When it has found me, it knows
That it's arrival has been written and recorded
In the villas of this world
Engraved in blooming decor,

In the neck of this civilization
'That' is the equivalence of a human baby
Whose attraction is unequivocal in unsurpassed pull
Spreading around sinless divine air
Has fallen down by the strike of no-promise of growth
And pondering
Amazing world!
Holding tight in the chest
The mechanical lifeless mercenary civilization
Is running after advancing competition,
I'm fallen on the floor maze bed
In the hope of competition to uplifting humanity,
In competition-less uncompetition
Has taken ally after the decay,

November 11, 2005
Glen Oaks, Queens
New York

All These Grieving Hearts

Bengali: Aishob Shukattopto Redoy

This sobbing and cry will stop one day
This grieving heart, at the demise of dear ones
After crying out again and again-
Shall calm down at one time with the strength of consolation
Slowly days will pass by
In the dark body of the night
With the promise to wake up the sun,
The overwhelmed heart and soul by the grief of losing someone
Will forget that dreadful time
The hardness of the strike will diminish away
The grieving heart slowly will take transform
Into the room of brightened space of memories-,

Now, it's not the overwhelmed heart soaked in cry
Now, it's the bright floating appearance of memories
Now, it's not the turmoil in the heart
Now, in silence it's the plucking of the memories
Spoken words, laughter, the alive incidences of dear ones
Come out alive in between times
Slowly the presence of those awaken memories
Like that hazy fading keeps fading away
At a distant horizon-Some stays, some gets faded
Some gets lost in the foggy light
In the endless body of vacuum of the creator-,

Deprived Solicitation

Now, the grieving heart again and again
Does not get overwhelmed sequestered with breathing
Now, from the gulf of the ocean like the vast quiet bed of water
The heart in nonflow meditation going silently
The inside's restless storm does not exasperate anymore-,

That child who is swinging in the swing
With affectionate touch of the parents
He'll grow up as well, the same way will swing
His own child-
They also in that grieving heart
Smoldering the clouds of memories of their dear ones
Slowly shall alleviate like the ocean's sleepy quiet water
At the unpredictable call of time
All cries, all grief, all heart wrenching sounds
Gradually shall float away in the invisible horizon of far distant
In there, slowly shall gather all memories
In the own courtyard of God closer to him-,

All these grieving souls in their journey to the eternal path
All shall go away, only will stay
Those gathered vessels of memories in the sky vacuum
This nature shall stay holding that vessel
Only it will be transformed at the signal of the creator
Towards another vast world.

November 15, 2005
Port Washington, L.I.

On The Tip of Thinking

Bengali: Vubnar Puruvagay

Once in a while a crazy thought
Gets on ride
This crazy mind,
Nearby, at distances, in our own
Bangla land
Unwanted pain and oppression upon helpless general people
The toppled overcrowded injustices by government bodies
Could be fixed with one slap
In difference of one month by sitting in power
This thought come running
Sitting in the back of flying horse,

The wretched people of Palestine land
Age after age
Oppressed by force of power,
The growth of terrorism where has rooted in
Like the industry of injustices in the conflict of this region
Have manufactured all kinds of worthy fertilizers
Scattered in this land, that's why-
In the tide of time
Have generated the birth of
Blossomed buds in the name of terrorism
That which kind has taken spread throughout the world
Where the toppled and forceful injustices of power
Have no boundary-,

Striking a heavy slap
At the root of all these problems
The mind wants to fix the boundaries
By posting
The signal wall of the creator
Whom there will be no way to disregard
On the part of unjust power groups
The hated diplomatic maneuvers,

The common people who only in the name of people
Would have been known and saved everywhere
In both shores-
Not by identifying
The indomitable sign of division in the name of religion,

The cordoned nets of injustices only would have been marked
Upon identification, would have been sent to deportation
This such strike of crazy thinking
Positioning throughout the world
All the smacked pieces as though dead on the ground
The such erected mountain of the evil power
Would have been diminished.

December 6, 2005
Glen Oaks, Queens,
N.Y.

The Slash of the Name Development

Bengali: Unnoyon Namaer Chabook

If it could be thought of
What kind of living is this-!
Cordoned all around with steel gates
That has started from the main entrance gate
In every step, in verandah, a surrounded scenario
The keys of developed civilization
The sign of sharp watch on life
Or, In other words, maybe the excess of post independence developments
Has made the life unbearable as such,
Due to the excessive pressure of lack of security
The pleasureful life from the open hut
Has taken shelters inside the surrounded gates
This is the life after so called claims of developments,

In different corners of the capital, especially
In big cities-
The value of life is equal to chained up captives
In Bangladesh the claim of developments resembles
The welcome presence of this picture-,
Right on the nose tip of law
In the face of injustices, crimes, atrocities and forceful dominations
The value of life only

Is equal to utmost try
To keeping alive, staying alive each day
Like the lottery, to counting the days of not gotten hurt-,

If it could be thought of
Is this the life?
The free life of a free country!
The security of worry free life, Where are you?
Not enough in foods and clothing, not plentiful
Let it be-
Heard that there came some developments
At minimal, free movement and peaceful sleep
That's a must
At least in this independent country!
All the power sharing political parties, all the governments
You have snatched away justices and have given injustices
At the end, snatched the free movement in the streets and sleep
You alone yourselves are drumming the development-whip noisily.

December 8, 2005
Port Washington, L.I.
N.Y.

Turbulent Language

Bengali: Proloy Vasha

Now, the darkness has landed slowly
The ever dazzling casinos of wealth and exuberance
The small clubhouses of intoxicate lovers
Will gradually wake up now-
In the startled fun room of brightness with colored bulbs
Some are on the top of roaring waves, intoxicated
Will doze in utter restlessness,
Some will build up mine of wealth
In scattered lands, and highlands-

At one side in the slowly engulfing darkness
Like the humming noise of groups of bumblebees
Is the assemblage of wealthy and riches
At other side in the advancing darkness
In the dwellings and cottages of helpless poor and have not's
It's the deep cold night of uncertain fate,
Wealthiness and poverty
The cruel reality of abundance and littleness
The throwing away of wasted foods in dumpsters
The uneasy hesitation of picking foods from garbage dirt,

Now, the darkness has landed slowly
In different horizons of this planet
Some are still in the fountain stream of light
Some, at an instant are in the shore of darkness

Deprived Solicitation

In that vast chest of this presence are gathered
In all horizons, two opposite pictures of reality
They are unknown to each other
A perfect union of all different languages and skin colors
Attached to the same tune in languageless language,

Now, the language of darkness slowly and quietly
Shall wake up talking
Assuming the identification of their own respected positions/locations,
It will be seen from behind the scene
The letters of bright name of renowned civilization
Perhaps in thoughtfulness
Shall bend the head to shy away
In thought pretending to be unmindful.

December 13, 2005
Greenville, Long Island
N.Y.

The Shameless Utterance

Bengali: Nirlojjo Uchharon

Sitting on the top of civilization, if
The bottom of it could be viewed
It will be seen-
The life of world human and the value of humanity
Sold in conscious mind
In inhuman tactics and actions
In the political auction of the world diplomatic market,

The roads and paths of this place
Are built of multiple colored human live bodies
For those who are in search of these paths
That which are assembled in lifeless slabs,
This is not a thunderbolt of any wicked planet
They're the people of this planet in appearance, in color
Only the activities are tied to the inhuman tone,

Those who are oppressed, not they
Those, whose life and family have been ruined, not they
Those who are the lock and keys of this destruction
They're the only pride boosters and their voices are loud
They're the ones only who claim to love life
As if, loud mouthing fits only them
They play destroying games with other people's life,
They who are the vulture-nails of destroying numerous lives
Whereas, how deeply cruel is this parade of claims,

By destroying the lives of innocent helpless humans
They themselves turn to be pride boosters
In loud mouth and they monopolize to be the owner of loving life
And that others love death
Even the serious hypocrisies would hide head in shame
In a distant darkness
To this internationally shameless claim.

January 7, 2006
Port Washington, L.I.
NY

To Want To Get

Bengali: Chaua Paua

The greetings of changing seasons I love
The mind craves to see
How many different kinds of touch come to play along
In each change of season
Noting the occurrence of their respective month,

The monotony of the same season
Does not excite the mind as much
This mind wants change-
But yet, not change of everything
The scenarios of sunrise and sunset
Bring the difference of feelings of different day value
Like the coming attraction of touching life little by little,

Here after, in the next scenario
Slowly and quietly winter comes as well
I want it too-
Want to see in my mind its touch as well
But yet, the welcome of too much cold does not hold in mind
Want it too but not in excessive fashion
A general winter like winter in Bangladesh
Or, some sprinkling of snows majestically from the sky
That's it, nothing more than that-
In branch after branches of trees
The touch of extra ornamental beauty of snow
The aroused stirring lust of desire for the beauty
Waking up once consoles the heart
That's it, not more than that of cold season,

That's the way I wanted all the season's
Impressions, coming and going in luxury
Yah! The spring, it's approach
Is the arousing of bursting heart
The touch of season through incessant flow of rains
It's the song of breaking the sleep of the grain's buds,

I wanted the summer too in full heart
All that luster lights that are spread around
But not the destructive killer storm
It's not welcomed in embracing mixed taste of seasons
Who will stop the fierce paw of its turbulent speed
That you're but an unprepared play of a delightful sphere,

I've wanted with all my heart and soul
The very sensitive foot-touch of all seasons
Still why then the destruction comes
Along with the seasons-,
that are Surrounded by the binding love,

What a glorious example administration of the creator
The one that is likable whose existence
Arouse in heart the flow of pleasure
To achieve that comes along
More unwanted unnoticed bunch of elements.

January 8, 2006
Glen Oaks, Queens
N.Y.

The Splashing Scratch Mark

Bengali: Bichhurito Dug

While working with pencil and paper
In the white page of the paper
A pencil scratch mark took effect
Amidst the clean surrounding suddenly-
This mark
Was not giving a good feeling at all,

Sitting in this clean page
As if occupied
That this unwelcome mark will pain the mind
Is never a doubt,
Whereas if it is left out untouched
It'll not get wiped out by its own,

The same way it'll remain seated in the whiteness
Whose influence is dirty
In a clean surroundings-,

The repeated erasing work by eraser
Shall be needed upon that mark
If the normal look of a clean place
Has to be brought about like that of before,

Because of dedicated try by the eraser
The mark gets faded and erased
From the occupied seated place
But again, some markings it seems

Many a time
Stays unclear foggy,
Visible, and not visible again
Just like being drawn and be afloat again,

The complete removal depends on
How much deep the scratch dug in
In this smooth page, and
How much devotion was given to erase that mark,
How high quality the eraser was?

The extinction of that mark shall be written in accurate
Upon the clear revelations of those reasons,
In page after page of human society
The presence of such scratch marks
Have no boundary, no end
Stay surrounded, nevertheless without try.

January 13, 2006
Port Washington, L.I.
N.Y.

The Sign of Decay

Bengali: Obokhoyer Obotar

Body adds up to human, human to society
Society adds up to each others to make this planet
Health degrades upon arrival of diseases in the body
It's necessary then, to diagnose
The reasons of sickness,
Only then the path of getting better
Take entrance into happiness,
When a disease appears in the body
Instead of treating by securing the reasons of the disease
Building of walls and barricades surrounding the disease spot,

Or-

Creating different kinds of obstacles
Shall not help to cure that disease
And there shall be no treatment either of human body
Sufferings shall effect the human society and this Earth of the
planet,
Taking steps according to conditions means
Not creating obstacles in leading life and body
It's thus indispensable to diagnose and treat the disease-,

Not finding the real reasons and Only blindly-
Incorporating of different kinds of medicines
Shall not be the right treatment
As a result-
Engulfing the symptoms of disease, the disease itself

Shall spread out extensively in the human body
Implementation of any obstacle right and left
Shall wound the body
The disease shall stay foot untouched to harm the body,

In human society in this earth of the planet
Similar to this so much injustices and oppressions
Staying spread at the root of societies
Terrorism and the forceful oppressions and torture of power
All those reasons are numerous in pages,
These injustices and oppressions all are the diseases of the body
The same way-
Whose right treatment after determining the reasons
Are the only ingredients to save the human and the society,

By not doing this and instead, creating all kinds of barricades
Shall be like the story of garrulous talking
Disease will remain only stones will be thrown
In wrong places unnecessarily-,
It'll be only pretending to treat disease
The diplomacy of world politics
Shall be a waste of unbelievable deceptions
It'll be the waste of human life, waste of time
Let that human sufferer be from

Any race or religion
It'll be a joke of the power of the civilized of civilization
The sign is only the decay of humanity.

January 27, 2006
Greenville, Long Island
N.Y.

Careful To Cross
This Slippery Path

Bengali: Shubdhunay Perute Hobay
Aitookoo Pichchill Poth:

High mountain,- the aches, grief and sorrows of deprived and have not's
Have accumulated here and became dense,- dazzles
At the reflection of scorching sun light -.
It takes the appearances of sharply slippery with revolting heat
And oppressed shouts as if wants to burst out.

When the burning heat of soul becomes unbearable
Pain and sorrows come down the body of mountain
Continuously -
Gradually melts down the accumulated innerself-cry
In the shape of crying water -,
And rolls down to the main public thoroughfare, still shiny and bright-
The wealthy and aristocratic cars become startled
At the sight of this dazzling fluid,-bring down the speed
And become very awaken and cautious -
Lest they fall upside down in this slippery path of sorrow and pain.

While going, they perhaps look back up for a moment
The dazzling white reflections of pain and sorrows
Make their eyes feel dizzy,
The humanity soul of civilization slowly turns foggy
Only then, turn their eyes quickly away -,

A shiver of fear peeps through their mind.
In the twinkling of their thought they encounter uncomfortable frenzy
Must cross this little slippery path,-they murmur
Carefully very carefully.

March 13, 1981
Brooklyn, NY

Are They Human!

Bengali: Era Ki Manoosh

Are they human ! Do their life
Has any value at all to Western World!
They are not human, rather, up in the middle of two legs
A heart was placed that walks !
They are in Bosnia, in Palestine country,
They are Lebanese, in the guise of minority in India,
They are a kind of life (creature), the hunger of Somalia,
They are not Iraqis' under oppression of queer.

The proud civilization of America and Europe and
In it's glass lens, they are human like
Transparent figures in the ridicule tapping of intension & gesture
They could be played around for nothing on self whimsicality.
Who says they are dying because of pain of oppression,
They are like a tool to test-run amusing tests
The same way you can do with mosquitoes
By pressing them between finger-tips & breaking apart their whole
intestine

They are not human that they will feel pain !
Never,- in the Europo-American civilization
Even the dogs and cats are more human,
Live in much adore and affection,
To their hungry tongue and greedy look
Who can give trouble, they sleep in the bed
Lick in the cheek of their masters
And give loving kisses in the naked lips of civilization.

These are- their human; in care, in pleasure
They are full to brim, breathe in the smell of meat
Their separate fresh foods are attractive to the eyes
The bonie-bodied people of so-called uncivilized nations
Could have been living such is the taste of look,
The civilized dog sleeps in the fat of peace.

Bosnia, Palestine, Lebanese and so more
Are they human? Let that be known.
Like toy-foam of America and Europe-:,- in their blow
They whirl around in twisted bangle,
They axe like insignificant animals, the civilized cats & dogs
Are much more human compared to them.
And wealthy oil miner of Middle East
Licks the tail of the civilized

August 6, 1993
Port Washington, New York

Passing This Way

Bengali: A Pothe Jate

So many times, I thought, While passing this way
That I'll sit by this bank
Some morning when crows are cawing
And when the water recess with fallen tides.

So varieties of stones and remnants of their bodies,
On some, algae have drawn it's color impressions
Some have sprinkles of sands, some have spots
Some have droplets of water sticking to their bodies.

I'll collect all these kinds while limping over, walking slowly
Lest my feet get tainted with algae-mud and sands,
Lots of variety shells scattered around besides stones
Broken are their faces and bodies and their beauty faded.

So many days, I thought
Stepping on these sands, stones, shells and water sprinkles scattered
I'll walk down far away where
Down tide ends and the continuity of water proceeds to endless streams.

Lots of stalks, seagulls come and sit in this broad sphere,
In the morning glare of sun light
They gently caress their wings with their beaks
Some walk dancingly polite catching the eyes to admire.

So many times, I thought, having seated at this bank
I'll swallow the enchanting feelings of water touching floated

Deprived Solicitation

Innumerable boats and on their bodies
The embracing beauty of morning sun with the intimate reflections
of water.

So many days, I thought, the beauty of this path
Has to be entrenched under my feet in cool touch
Into my body and then to be engraved into my heart
While walking on the sands stones and their remnants through
collection of pleasure

I only keep passing this way
Over and over again in this path
Have no leisure only thought comes back again and again
The more I think, the hope only remains in sea-sand of thoughts.

September 26, 1997
Port Washington, NY

Perseverance

Bengali: Shudhona

My, this perseverance walks along
Under lemon tree, Shimul. Polash, the Mudhobi Lota
Climbing down their deserted hearts through
The yellow garden of luxury of the evening. In the bank of green-
The rose, Mollika, Muloti, Jasmine flowers
In their helpless timid softness,
On the roof tin-sheds where leaves are engaged in friendships,
Where full-moon light is driven away with the engulfing moonless
darkness.

In the raw smells of fresh leaves of jute plant fields
In the wave of green paddy fields with golden crops peeping through
The persons who walk down the midst of these in agony with burden
of poverty
My perseverance walks along with their breaths.

In the villages, markets, in the stoves of countless human
The heartfelt pain of insufficient foods in the covered pots
From the cooking of which come out the visible vapors
That, in disguise, gives the consolation of real hope of plenty of foods
In the hungry curious looks of their children,
The past healthy body that walks now towards village markets
Showing the number of ribs in their bodies, a sign of fruits of post-
indepence rules,
Come back from the market with half empty baskets in their hands,
My perseverance round and around
Returns at the site of their existence.

In the center of Indra of my perseverance, the lightning sound of
longing echoes--
If even, a green leaf can be saved
From being becoming yellow-,
If even a yellow leaf
Could be kept alive from being dead dropping,
If even, a pillar could be protected
From being attacked by the deadly termites--,

If this very moon light of this very nation
Could be carried to each home, even a drop of it--,
If with the full touch of this rain
A very little bit of pain of innumerable human
Could be alleviated-,
Then, at least, one drop full of weight of this sea of pain and sorrows
Will become lesser from the load full burden of mankind.

October 3, 1997
Long Island,
New York

Notes: Shimul,Polash,Mudhobi Lota,Mollika, Muloti = Different kinds of
enchanting
smelly flowers.

Jute plant = At one time golden fiber plants of the world, now mostly replaced by
artificially developed rayon's, fibers..etc.

Your Order

Bengali: Tomar Uddesh

One day in that vacuum in the blue sky
By drawing the surroundings of thrilled supernatural bindings
The way the shape-engulfed personality body of 'MUFASA'
Came floating into the clouds- ,

If you yourself likewise, suddenly with bodied-soul
Would have appeared covering the sky with finger pointing,
The drifting trend towards the doom of this mankind worldwide
May have been saved.

Perhaps the sharp directives of your finger,
The order reflections would have brought wisdom
At the root of this society, in the brain kingdom of rulers.

If that wouldn't have been enough in this ignorant villa
I was always ready-,
From that time in the past
Waiting for your order.
I would have engraved at the root of all encampments of injustices
Your order that is dissolution less over eternal peaks.

March 20, 1997
Long Island, New York

Notes: MUFASA-- Actor hero of 'Lion King' movie

Test

Bengali: Por1kkha

Ok, Go ahead
Finish thyself,
What it is to burn yourself like husks
To draw the end of oppressed heart,
Instead, what a thrill it is to shut the life suddenly!

I told you--
These are all rats, termites and cow dung worms
The healthily grown flies and mosquitoes in dirt nourishments
Will sit in your body and flash
And will suck your juice out in comfort, tear you off and eat
Like homeless hungry vultures
The hope of your life.

I told you--
These are low cadre tonsured dogs,- suddenly
Coming out of bush
They are like frenzied running wild foxes,
Like heat strickened swirling
Lunatic stray -dogs of the street-
Your hopeless vigor, weak from all-lost body and mind of yours
They will bite out even the last support of your life.

I warned you--
Don't go ahead with very little defense at your hand,
The easily gotten heap of flash
And accumulated severe foul smelled magnetic attraction

Has hooked them up into addiction
Like nothing could resist them.

With one sudden paw they will drag you down
To the bottom of that life-killer fouled-smelled heap
You may never sense the place of your existence.

I told you--
These society-destroyer worm people
Are crazy for the blood
Of the poor, the middle class, school going class, the general people.
Irrespective of nation, age, society and religion
In the safe haven of security of the rulers
Many of these have tunnel like connections,
As though, the line of ants with diamonds in their mouths
Enter into the hidden hole underground.

Nop! All these terrible consequences
The prayer and warning of engulfed burned soul
The blazing licking tongue of fire of the darkness
And the bitter pain of their poisonous bites
Nothing could stop you!

I urged you don't go, beware-
In this battle you will loose your person and your life,
You smiled silently and politely, leaning down-
With heavenly brightness in your eyes and face
Not caring the fear at all!

I shivered with pride and dignity
Lava-tears burst out of my eyes
With eternal respect towards your turbulent look
With directional blessings of guiding stars.
In fact it was not meant to stop you
It was only a test for you from me.

August: 1, 1997
Port Washington, New York

The Greatest Mother
Of Hearsay

Bengali: Kingbodontir Shera Ma

The 'Nobel' of the Academy is lean and small
Upon the sky high person of yours--,
Our all out words of undertakings
That we have bestowed upon you
From all shore of human races
The Nobel prize of all our hearts,

(In memory of Mother-Teresa)

Septemeber 19.1997
Long Island, New York

In The Guise Of A Friend

Bengali: Bondhu Sheje

You are a friend, whereas flooded with greed in your heart,
Squeezing the whole body of mine
Like the udder of a cow you want to suck out
All my nutritious life-strength.

Upon gotten cut my vein
The stream of blood that flows,
To satisfy your thirst you are anxious to the brim
To pour down that whole flow into your throat.

You know, that will finish me,
Whereas you pretend as guise of a friend
That,- it is nothing--
Only then, you will divide and grab my body
In the cover of coating of many scenarios of Upstream Farakka's
Designed contracts and it's sweet definitions.

You thought I would not know,
Would not understand your flawless deceitful strike,
I'm not a lost-mind non-understanding ruler-machine,
I'm a life thriven vigilant guard of crores of voices, crores of minds

September 23,1997
Long Island, New York
Notes:
Farakka-The Farakka. dam built by India off-shore of North-West of
Bangladesh

Neglected Death

Bengali: Obohelito Mritto

This is the way you embrace death,-- you
In the headline of news papers
Become picture of news -
May be not even that--.

Being chained up in the repeatedly licking thrust of blazing death,
In every day news
In the curious eyes of the early morning
You become the news of talk.

That's all -,

Within the difference of couple of days
You get lost
From the page of news,- gradually
From the minds of compassionates,
And the minds of the rest in advance
Keep awaiting to forget.
With you goes the history of your neglected life
In the welcome house of God-

After that -,

The cold eclipse of long waited death
Guards your children, wife and your parents
The dependent family members
With a hand-wave of sympathy,

And embraces, then, into the soundless nights
Of unknown swing of difficult breathing --.

As you swing, at one time
These of you become tired in your eyes
And get leaned at the back of the swing,
Then you go faded gradually and get lost in silence
From the familiar faces of the society, the roads, the path
From the familiar house, surroundings -,

The active society, the rulers, ruling courts even by mistake
Did not look back !

(Thoughts on the deaths in the blaze of a garments factory in Dhaka,
Bangladesh)

August 9, 1997
Long Island, New York

Humanity Detached From The Stalk Slowly Coming Down

Bengali: Numchey Dheray Brintocchuto Munobota:

I see snow storm falling down from the sky
Like a dream of eternal fountain,
Sometimes it's like cotton
Sometimes woolen grain.
It does not appear that the sky has broken apart,-only
Floating and falling non-stop,

Suddenly gets speed by the slap of the wind
Solemn nature all around,
As if the aberration of humanity
Coming down detaching from the stalk,-thereafter
Lying on the body of ground or like coral hill.

Strongly held in the clutch of my three fingers
My pen and from its spine
Blue blood like running arrow
Aimed through the air,- then
In the paper
Getting alliance in composing words.

I see snow storm--
Like humanity slipping through the body of civilized sky in Bosnia..
In different habitations of Africa
Here and there in the Middle East, in Chechnya
In the poor areas of underdeveloped and developing nations of
Asia,
Worldwide in the black, brown and white's
Unhealthy living homes of slums,
And country after country refined political torture
Upon the chest of general populace.

I see snow is falling--
The definitions of human values are closing shut and
Scattering around in front of my eyes,
Filing hills of snows, inches, feet and even more
Feet are measuring upwards,
Ridiculing the developments of the civilization,
Scattered human races
With no foods, hungry, half-fed, taking the tastes of malnutrition
as they live
Without treatments pass weeks months
Like the snow fall in scattered flash of beam.

Snow is falling defeating fifty years of history
This January of Nineteen Ninety Six
Has broken all the records
Like cottons in the guise of snow flakes,
For the committed welfare of all humans, the degraded inches of
humanity
Is growing up, as though.
Like the snow fall all over the world.
Developments of civilization should be alike
For all human beings

Deprived Solicitation

Like it is in the palaces of wealthy and well to-do
Unto the hungry homes and habitations of the poor & unfortunates.

I see snow falls detaching from the stalk of humanity dripping down
the tormented steps
And filing up around me,
Experienced strikes of the crowbar
Making it file up high here and there disregarding the general rules
Like the shots from destructive cannons,
The weariness of deprived and neglected humanity still
Filing up in the old places
Only to draw attention of proclaimed civilization
In the hope of getting a little touch of affection and mercy.

January 17,1996
Manor Sands Pharmacy
Port Washington, New York

This Life This Pain

Bengali: Aei Jibon Aei Betha

When the good-buy took it's effect
It is more than two decades now,
In a clean pellucid body of mine came down then
Feelings of pain alleviated pure consolation
In depth of my mind the transcends of fright has taken exit.

I am relieved and alive
This was the conclusion of my clean-cut thought.

Back it came to-day
The pain of society with the pain of my vein
Has taken alliance.
I want to have pain alleviated conclusion
I would like to see that the spark of my pain
With the pain that is engraved in the back and lap of society
Has taken leave forever.

My mind wants to get relief and live
By removing and dispelling the starvation of crores of people all over
I want to see
In a highly pleased celestial ray of splendor
Seated I am.

And they -
Are in full bloom in the cheerful triumph-song of life
Are no more worried and preoccupied in the thoughts of foods,
clothes & shelters
Are not pounded, smashed and bruised in befallen thoughts
They are also alive and living well.

December 28, 1996
Long Island, New York

Nonetheless, You Came

Bengali: Tobu, Tumi Ashechilley

Your wondrous world now, is,
In an extra-mundane celestial environment beyond human knowledge,
Created by God's own hand
In overwhelmed eternal garden of sweet aroma.

The fever-sicks, troubled with sorrows and misery of this bank
The befallen sickly distressed lives that lie on the roads
Hungry, neglected, the bony bodied
Have become deprived from your affectionate motherly touch
For ever--.

For so long, these unfortunate mourning souls
Having enjoyed the care affection and nursing of your motherhood
Have engaged themselves, out of habits, in remorse hope
That, without you, even two moments wouldn't do.
That we have got to lose you
The simple open minds of these afflicted health's
Didn't think a moment of this unforgivable truth.

Nevertheless, you came-
Loved these neglected human
You have given the full moonlit love
The body and mind of your whole existence throughout your life.

Nonetheless, you have touched these
Suffering souls, ill misery leprosy's hands,
Have given them consolations,
The taste of life of a human being.

Nonetheless, you have come-
Sat next to them holding their hands,
Picked them up in your lap,
Have given in the ear to ear of hearts
That attachment of hearts-
Have commended, witnessing the human sufferings-
I leave behind with my nursing tearful heart
The salvation of human,
That's why you are the life mother of world's suffered humanity.

Nevertheless, you came-
irrespective of caste creed and color
With the blessings of God
At our shore-
We submit to that in tearful eyes
And we are blessed.

(In memory of Mother Teresa)

September 13, 1997
Manor Sands Pharmacy
Port Washington, NY

Now At Sleep The Beautiful Parakeet

Bengali: Akhon Akhon Ghumonto Shundor Parakeet

So small a bird whom in the palm of a hand
Could be retained in playful pleasure,
So small a life whom in the palm of a hand
Could be held in the name of act of play,
So small a body whom in the palm of a hand
Could be covered completely in the lap of hide and seek.
Green in color awake all time in the myth of life,
In the cage all different kinds of acrobatic activities
Excite a silent pleasure in the skilled playhouse of nature.

That all these good feelings, love and sinless pleasure
In this toy-play of nature gives an impeccable flow of heart,
Suddenly, the dying-sick and the pleasure kingdom falls in
Pin drop silence
Held in the hand the lifeless body of a life-full heart
The fruitless prayer of passionate outburst that this has to be saved,
Has to be kept alive this beautiful life that held in hand.
So small a body, it seems, anything could be done,
This is so nothing, whereas helpless human with all it's wisdom
Goes head-down in mental agony into the palm's lifeless beauty.

January 26,1993
Port Washington, New York

Note. Parakeet-- A kind of bird

Birthday Celebration

Bengali: Jonmodiner Utshow

Since the dawn of spring or even before that
Countless blooming times
Have passed by-
The accosting birthday cake ever didn't hold
The light of candles.

The time has come climbing down the seasons steps
And has gone with the pulling of tide,
The resurrection of birthday did never happen in close vicinity.

The work full life walking over the body of life
Has made me forget the count of birthdays,
I have survived and am surviving
From the morning east-horizon I only pulled the grinder
To the setting horizon of the West untiringly.

To-day suddenly you all, by catching me in birthday celebration melee
Has brought shame upon my whole person,
I in the company of millions of birthday less homes
Was the light of lightless,
In whose homes the usurer walks, or-
Who with their children are quietly helpless and hopeless
Whose only hope is to pull their lives relentlessly.

September 14, 1996
Port Washington, New York

Color Differentials Wakes Up Under Obsession

Bengali: Obsessionay Jaggay Utthay Borno Boishommo

I thought, Sitting in the intimate womb of civilized world
I'll pass the time, the thought of clash among human then
Will bid good-buy in the oblivion.

All around is only prologue of amity
Fragrances of Otto, roses resounding in the air,
the skin color,- it's horror and tremor
Will fade away from the melee of the society,

The merriments of civilization in the air all over
By the right,by the left, in the back of human,
In the corner here and there of social groups,
Distracted exultations and summations of expressions everywhere,
The revolting strike of color still
Did not fade away,
Division wakes up in the human shore
With all hopes and aspirations and their fulfillments being achieved
In the sitting shore of these proud civilizations.

The capable and famous American Footballer O.J. Simpson implicated
Double murder case becomes monstrous looking
In every nerve of the society
In the unadulterated tide of all human

Deprived Solicitation

In the court, in the published photos & in the media excited magnetic
reports,
The pierced impression of skin color carry away
The equality and balance of opinions in the wooden box of justice.

T.V. and News Media's unworthy
Excessively implied meaningless importance of war-trumpet
Tored off the silent cover of skin color differentials.
T.V. robs rates
Human gets hunger of hyenas !

The activities of social values, welfare, the hot news of Clinton
Administration
Get sunk throughout the Country the year round,
Awake only O.J. Simpson in every way.

Imposed by the media on the neck of society
The blind addicted disarray impassionate outburst of human
Run after Nicole Simpson, Ronald Goldman and
O.J. Simpson's case under seize of obsession.

An incorporeal voice echoes in the air
Is media for human, or
Human is for the media
Time has come to think over.

April 16,1997
Long Island, New York.

Halted Faded World

Bengali: Stubbdo Biborno Prithibi

A small canal, over it is a bridge of wooden plates
It's width would be about four feet
In this side (west) is a living house
Built as a Bungalow,

Erected in a beautiful surrounding
In the front pond is a long wide concrete build wharf (ghat)
In it are the playhouses of all kinds of fish
Further to the right (west) is a bigger pond, another luxury,

On the other side of the bridge a narrow path started
After passing a few houses in either side
It falls in the entrance boundary of town- bazaar
This after, bazaar markets, town noisily rose up,

The monsoon seasons water hyacinth and water
Have overwhelmed to the brim underneath
In the long run length of the bridge
The shaky conditions of the weak bridge, some wood plates missing,

At goodbye time, standing in the middle of the bridge
Mind is dwindling, bridge is shaking
Turning around I'm bidding goodbye
To the very dearest person of my heart,

Deprived Solicitation

She is standing at the gate of bunglaw, pregnant
Hands in the gate-door panel tears in eyes
First time in life while bidding goodbye
That I've seen tears in her eyes,

The mind unknowingly in pain and fear
Became engulfed-
And yet, I bade goodbye
In her eyes tears of sorrow but why?!

The answer came on the tip of a month
Receiving the news of her sickness in the language of telegram
I'm returning through the thoroughfare of Dacca
The world seemed had faded,

The red traffic lights as if
Holding the time for ages
Not allowing to proceed, distance increasing-
The speed of the rickshaw is slowing down unnoticed!!

(In Memory of my dear Bubu (sister) in 1969)

November 10, 1997
Long Island, New York

Keep On Watch

Bengali: Kheale Rakho

You became rich in wealth
And in respect as well, maybe not
Doesn't matter, continue growing richer
This aim is awake in everybody's life,

The play of fate and the harvest of hard work
For everyone, by the same rule
Doest not happen in this hard-pressed life
Some crosses over some fall behind
In this test in the previous surroundings the same way,

Be garlanded with wealth and enjoy, does not matter
Only, don't neglect those who are
Poor, who stay fallen behind
In the cycle of poverty
In the yearly book accepting the defeat of the day end hard work,

Your steps from downside
Has climbed up high, no matter, winning the hardship
You've come up at the peak point of this fourway road
Only, don't hate and don't hold contempt
Towards this poor half fed villa,

They've no fault of their own or maybe some
They stay fallen holding the wish of God on their head
Accepting the reasons of their conditions as the game of fate
Many of them do give try
But don't get harvest like that of your fruitful harvests,

Don't ridicule them upon their poor face
All devotions do not bear same fruits
Bring in memory of your past or your surroundings
If you could lift them by holding hands
Or yet, keep watch so this human don't sink to deep bottom,

Slight touch of pleasant dose of southern bridge
Let these poor humans enjoy, open up your heart
Look and see the world is smiling in greetings
Towards you, because they exist
You get cordial reception, you are at higher elevation.

November 3, 1997
Port Washington, L.I.
N.Y.

Witness

Bengali: Shakhi

The lives are walking, on the go
Downstairs on the concrete road,- up above is
Signs of scattered wounds are multilayered
In it's body-
Their appearance sometimes, suddenly
Appear horrifying in the dark-,

The earlier beauty of the leaves are gone by now
Few trees in burning sunray
Are standing as witness of the time-
These are orphans today,
They have donated the bones to the testimony of the age
With a hope to the fulfillment of tomorrow
What a tremendous strength in the lips of its mentality-,
Life-!

That man keeps walking to the eternal path
Slow speed in long steps,
From it's footstep climbing upwards-
The path of white layers on green dry grass
Adhering to the body of the hill
In a zigzag map of walking path-,

With the history of the trees
The history of the man, as if
Is attached in the same tune-,
Along the speed of the step

He keeps expressing history for the poet seated above-,
One or two concrete stones haphazardly
Run into and hurt
The feet of the traveler-,
They don't talk
And yet, let know their speech
In sudden strike or in the collision speed of the vehicles-,

The poet only keeps gazing
Opening the door of the heart
Holding the expression of their language
Spreading the album of time.

March 9, 1978
Chittagong
Bangladesh

Tool

Bengali: Hatiar

These people are play dolls
Only a tool,
To vote and to make King
To whom the throne is capsized,

At all other times opposite reactions
Who are the people,
Whose claims, to whom liable to answer
Come at voting time!

April 13, 1996
Port Washington, L.I.
N.Y.

Still Now

Bengali: Akhono

Whereas still, the mentally crippled vultures
Chew right and left the hopes of the Bangla cottages
Letting go the blind youth arms in hands
The decapitated education system in hands runs scattered in naked clusters
Knitting the duty of teachers in blood threads
The King's court vastly decorated in a political teacher's meetings,

Cherished that bringing the uprooted ruins of all those disarray and robbers
That I will save the vessel again of lost justices
Reestablishing the rule of truth and justices
I'll render my endured services in keeping the promise,

Whereas still, the inextinguishable arrow of hopes
With bow at hand that it will not miss the aim target
Counting the silent depressed dawn of burning husks
The ransacking of education binding in political mischievousness
Harangued a circus, piecing the fate of people
The self-seeking lords today turn into human lover bridegroom.

September 21, 1994
Port Washington, L.I.
N.Y.

In All These Stages

Bengali: Aishob Monchoshallai

Every day I keep getting killed
For this, there's no morning, afternoon or evening
These amazing stages have so very amazing killing tools,

The probable hope of morning awakening of the day
Or, of the invited pleasure-wandering guests of the evening
The sweet aroma of ata of the invitees where
Have made mixture of wonderful beauty of red and yellow colors
Like the both side of a special kind of rose petals,

In those places as well, in burned wisdom
I get killed regularly-
Keeping this 'air', my very dear close friend
As the witness-,

Because of its (air) quiet divine life giving nourishment
I come back to life after being killed again and again
In the stages of this world
Becoming the witness of oppressions
Upon the lives of general populace,-and
Baby, children, young, and youth alike.

June 30, 1997
Port Washington, L.I.
N.Y.

Want Relief From Pain

Bengali: Jontronar Uposhom Chai

Every flash, cell and mass of my body
Is flooded with strikes after strikes
The way the vultures-
From all around of a dead body
Snaps away the pieces of flesh and tissue
With the strike of their sharp beaks and nails-,

Upon the limbs of my body-, only

The flesh hungry jubilant dance is not there
Like those, at far distance up in the blue vacuum
No scenarios of vultures coming down in flocks
Covering the sky-Like the swarms of planes
Not seen in this kind of lunge of fangs-,

The torture of daily bites, as if-
Has numbed the nerve system,
In the endless flow of wariness drowsiness comes down
In the eyelids like that of senseless feelings
The oppression of ruler upon helpless innocent human
In the face of attack by high persecution and by injustices-,

Is thrown collectively in the world-houses,

They, often is captive in soundless shouting,
Seated and besieged upon my body and soul
I want relief from this lunge
I want to be free
I want to perceive even this little taste of human smile.

Junel, 1996
Port Washington, New York

My Fear

Bengali: Amar Voi

I don't fear your violent brandishing
You seemingly human lover of destroying nature
The huge paw of your mischievousness
I don't fear,-I know
You're exulted in destroying the hearts and lives, or
Becoming a definitive cause of their hardships and sorrows
You're delighted in the games of your own rules
Yet then, I'm firm and strong in my mind in fearless feet,

My fear is only
At their fallen silence, the quiet look of mother
And, at the self screaming in rolling tears,
My fear is that befallen human heart
Who tolerates the coldest snow and spends the night
In the corner of the footpaths in an indifferent smile,

And that one who in downwards face
Excusably passes by in feeble smile with indifferent mind
My fear is that sorrowful wild look
Who collects foods from the garbage in the street corner,

My fear is that loneliness
That silently passing of the neighbor like an unknown
That fear and mistrust towards the next person
That worm infested collective hesitation polarized in central consciousness
That seize-all conspiracy of surrounding modern comforts

Where human soul
Slowly falls at a distance from the core of feelings,

I fear the words "good weekend"
The only nourished desire of too much pressure
That buys out their mentality-
That blinds the power of judgment to look
That tears off the theme flow of thinking-, only
Their look is thrown on the weekend check,

My fear is this flatly fallen humanity
Their senseless apathy-,
Their foolish eyebrow raising pretending as good people
My fear is their-
Power of tolerance to deceive themselves,

In boiling words of storm, only
I feel like screaming-
I cannot stand the meaningless foolish power of yours
You go away, stand aside
Keep dying,- and yet
Don't suffocate the intolerance, let it live
Let it blossom in your garden
Face to face with rightful justice.

April 26, 1980
Brooklyn, NY

Unheard of Flood Strike, Homeland Devastated

Bengali: Ochrutopurbo Bonnar Aghate Jorjorito Shadesh

I have sold myself In a foreign living,-
As an immigrant, I've rendered here and there
The services of my labor,
Whatever wisdom, collection of educations-,
Towards the sick and ill population and
To the society as well, more or less
My family and for my own self
Towards living and maintaining a livelihood,

This is life!, sacrificing myself
I am in a wisdom burned unbearable
White pale sky courtyard,
Country cries, mother cries
The mother, motherland-
The two thirds of which is under water
Helpless, in bottomless blind islands
Floating, in the surrounding cryless, tearless
The soundless lives in dumbfounded utter surprise
Looking around,- they're floating
In the besieged trap of endless bottomless water,

Only once, once only,- only
For this time-
In a deep quiet prayer to stay alive,

A postal Thana, sixteen unions
In it, count now all the villages
Small town, bazaar, the rice mills and shops
All are floating, nowhere there is an island
Whom you could call a house, nowhere
There is a home whom you could call a house
Only, some parts in two side of a high bridge
Are over the water
This is the only dry land, an island
Its name is Hajigonj Island-
The rest of the town is underwater,

In this place the hut(bazaar) sits for the namesake
Some selling and buying for each day,
Whoever can come by boat in the hope
For some foods to bring to water floated home,
Those who have means to afford
This sprinkle of light is only for them
The rest stays unfed-
Day goes, night comes in rustling disappointment
They become silent witness-
Only fear keep touching them in vibrations,
Under the seize in vast unenduring water
Like the last ray of the day
This could not diminish them, because

They're dumbfounded, their senses have been numbed
By the weeping of the surrounding water,-

The two thirds of whole Bangladesh
Is a similar each individual surrounded Hajigonj Island,
Fearless are their inhabitance,

The held tight this Bangla in their chest out of love,
But this cruel strike of flood
Have recklessly ransacked their hopes and aspirations,

In every village and home the boundary of trees
Are standing up like floating over vast waters
In them the dear inhabitance
The dear people of everyday life
Whether alive or not-
There is no sign of it, no indication of it
Only scattered are one or two dingy boat
Keep awake in the curve of trees of village homes,

This vicious flood of nerve numbing strike of nineteen ninety eight
Two months passed by now
From the first day of flood,
Coming at the end, there is no home, no house
No dry land anywhere
It's as if impossible to live without touch of dear land,

Whirled in a deep desire in a foreign home
The conscience is confounded to the spin of a top
That I have sold myself In a foreign living!

Whereas, a solution of flood attack is a must, an all time solution--,

At the side of this endless wordless sufferings
Of my country people, my relatives and non-relatives
I could not offer any such consolation, any such help
The extended hand of mine from this shore of the horizon
Confined to a difficult restricted limit could not reach
At their suffered courtyard-,
And yet, I am awake-
The low light from the table lamp keep touching my forehead,
In front in the reflections on the mirror the lines in my forehead
Keep coming up floating-

In each of the line-
Bearing the witnesses of millions of afflictions.

(Dedicated in memory of dear Bangladeshi)
September 9, 1998
Port Washington, L.I. N.Y.

Occupancy

Bengali: Odishttha

When the pain shows up in me
In each part of my body, disease-like bites
Come afloat, because of squeezing
Body does not want to move in normal fashion-,

May I not even utter about my pain and hardship
To you-
And you don't even want to know, whereas
I cannot express it from my own either
In this kind of whirling net besieged is my talk and pain-,

The relief from pain in near time
Let be not attainable
I know I've to keep fighting in the lava of this pain
How long, how much in deep pain I don't know
And yet, wouldn't you give a chance to speak of the pain!

You stay occupying my kingdom
We the people have given you
That right-
Have installed this disgruntled
Mind luxury occupancy of yours
You're powerful in alliance with my voting right, a ruler
To safe guard me
I've bestowed upon you this ruling key
Yet then-
The talk of my pain, the expression about my body ache

Is meaningless to you
They will remain unspoken like suffocating to die,
You will not listen
You will not take responsibility to alleviate
By undertaking treatment-,

If, that is to be
What I need you for!
Sitting in my kingdom over my wealth
You will kill my own right,
You will suppress me
Throwing these hardships upon me
This is not what I want
Your occupancy is no longer allowed
Upon my body and mind.

December 19th 1998
Port Washington, L.I.
NY

Seldom

Bengali: Doibat

If at any such day, it happens
Meat, in their house-
Not in every week
Not in every month
Not even one day among these days,

Leaving the counting of days aside in default
Suddenly, if one day
The meat pot is placed on the stove
In their house, - We have to say
This day, in this house, is a celebration day,

The little boys and girls in joyous play
Have stirred up noisily, - In their house
Guest is coming, so to say
Meat shall be cooked, - perhaps
The aroma basmati rice shall be around as well,

Today is their delightful day
Among so many days that were passed
One this, is the memorable day
Meat shall be eaten-
In the name of guests, the gift of the day,

Inside the glittering of the city
It's not so called the house corner of the rich and wealthy
It's not the unused wasted foods of the wealthy of the world

M. Hasan Imam

In these twenty-five years of independence
Possibly sixty out of ninety percent people of village Bangla has this
kind of day,

Meat, even though, may not be the regular companion of their fate
They survive, human survives
Only the math stays imbalanced and unmatched
In the accounting book, manipulations
May not match the result in the rate of survival.

January 13th, 1998
Port Washington, L.I. NY

The Boy and Impression of Civilization

Bengali: Chaleti o Showotar Chup

Thoroughfare, a boy by the side of footpath
Crying, hands in eyes, as to
Wipe the wet eyes out of cry,
Seems, calling someone in the tune of cry
With the rhythm of breathing,
The shadow of a hawk came afloat brighter and then vanished
At far in the opening of the sky
With its floating body,

I came closer to the boy, others surrounding him
From all sides-One or two with the mind of passers' by
Casting a look at the boy unmindfully,
Another one throws a verse of consolations
In the air-
The boy is unchanged, storm of no peace in him,

In his wearing is a torn pant, naked body
Like the layer of dust of Bangla
Layers have settled in his body, my country!
Nobody would believe this body
Has touched water for many days
Country of water, Bangladesh, and he is her son!
Suddenly, the speed of a car I felt by the side
In it a burst of laughter

Needless to say towards the footpath, - not foreigner
I realized-
They're civilized, the blood of Bangladesh flows
In their veins-
They're of course worth ridiculing
To see and get amused and laugh
This is my country, naked
Poverty is its royal mark
Indecorous taunting is its civilized garments
My country-!

September 27th, 1970
Dhaka, Bangladesh

Language of Life

Bengali: Jiboner Vusha

Is devotion to eating the only worthiness of life?
If the language of life is this narrow and limited
I've then, no support for it at all
Standing at the peak of mountain at time of sunrise
I want to play the battle game-play
With the darkest black clouds and wanted to engrave there
The language of life is the service to humanity,

And more, I want to place there the song of exalted life
The high rise and fall of tune, the tide of joy at
The site of sweet melody of cuckoo
For the soul of human-
Only earning and sleeping is not the talk of life
Everything then, falls behind, the greatest creation becomes a joke.

June 10th, 1971
Dhaka, Bangladesh

M. Hasan Imam: Author

M. Hasan Imam is the son of Hajigonj, Chandpur (Cumilla), Bangladesh. He's an established Pharmacist in New York, a poet by nature, a novelist and a periodical writer. He currently has in '"his credit twenty two publications of poetries and novels. This is not the only identity he has. Since his youth he's been a successful organizer both in his motherland as well as in New York.

He's been living in New York for three decades. Here, along with a devotion to literature, he was engaged in writing periodicals in different Bengali newspapers on economic and political aspects of Bangladesh and its people. He started writing since school life and has collections since 1969. Around that time, his writings started to come up in some national newspapers in Dhaka.

He joined in the liberation war in 1971 as a freedom fighter against Pakistani invaders. He was at the time a Senior Officer in the Quality Control Department of Pfizer Laboratories International. He was praised in those times because of his devotion to the human cause, like recovering in a go-down of the looted items such as gold, utensils, cattle, houses, etc. after they were identified in the worst possible looted area during the war as the chairman of the Freedom Fighters Society, Hajigonj and returning them to the real owners with sentry guards after the downfall of the Pakistani army in December 16th, 1971. He did this for about four months before rejoining Pfizer. At the same time he was protecting the business institutions in Hajigonj from looting by providing around the clock sentry guard to those locations.

As a first batch student he earned B.Pharm (Hons) and Masters Degree in Pharmacy from Dhaka University, Bangladesh and got into the Ph.D. program at The University of Connecticut, Storrs Campus. After completing two years of course work and before starting research, due to financial hardships, he went back to New York and completed his R.Ph. in 1980.

- Before coming to the USA he performed his duties as Quality Control Manager of Pfizer Labs International from 1971-1973. Also performed as Chairman, Drama Committee of Pfizer Family and staged, for the first time, a Drama in Engineers Institute for 2 nights. It was very well received throughout various newspapers. Under his guidance as the Chairman of the Bengali Translation Committee all official documents were translated into Bengali and formatted for future use.
- In New York he worked as the Inventory Control Manager in Ketchum Laboratories and as Plant Manager in Emgee Pharmaceuticals, both located on Long Island, 1977-1981.
- Founding General Secretary and writer of the constitution of the Hajigonj Thana Student Society, 1963-1964.
- Founding General Secretary and writer of the constitution of the Dhaka University Pharmaceutical Society, 1966-1967. Dr. Habibur Rahman, a teacher of the dept, was the President of the organization.
- Founding General Secretary and writer of the constitution of Pharmacy Graduates Association (PGA), Bangladesh and a life sustainer as General Secretary through difficult times for five years, the Presidents were Mr. Wahed Ahmed, Managing Director of Fisons Pharmaceuticals, and Mr. Salimullah, Managing Director of Jasons Pharmaceuticals, among others.
- Actively engaged in establishing the constitution and the organization of Bangladesh Pharmaceuticals Society after independence, before which it was Pakistan Pharmaceuticals Society, 1972
- President and General Secretary of the Bangladesh Society, New York, 1979-1984.
  Involved in activities for about twenty years serving the Bengali community and the author of the accepted and approved full-pledged constitution of the Bangladesh

Society, as the chairman of the constitution committee, in 2001, which he started working on in 1979.

- Chairman, FOBANA Constitution Committee and the author of the full-pledged FOBANA constitution.
- Author of the constitution of Farrakka International Committee, New York.
- Founding General Secretary and President of Bangladesh Forum of North America for eight years, and the author of its constitution, as chairman of the constitution committee, 1987 and up.
- He is the creator of the Evergreen famous name, the 'Embassy Building' located on Highland Avenue in Jamaica Queens, 1979. In those days this was the only building with the highest concentration of Bangladeshis at one location after the Bangladesh Embassy.

  That's how he started addressing the building and writing in society's magazines and eventually, it got the name in 1979.
- He was one of the main personalities to organize a demonstration in front of the United Nations under the banner of the Bangladesh League of America in 1973 for repatriation of Bangladeshi POWs and civilians who got held up in Pakistan after the Liberation War in 1971.
- He was the energy and main organizer to form the Committee for Democracy in Bangladesh outside the platform of Bangladesh Society, New York to organize a protest in front of the United Nations against the invitation of the then military ruler Ershad Hossain to speak in the upcoming general assembly of the United Nations in 1982.
- While a Ph.D. student at UConn, Storrs, he was the president of international students at International House, director of which was Dr. Knapp at that time.